TALES OF AN AMERICAN LESBIAN

The Best of the Straight & Narrow: 1986 - 1993

HOLLY VALERO

Tales of an American Lesbian: The Best of the Straight and Narrow • 1986 - 1993
Copyright © 2020 by
Holly Valero

This book is a work of fiction. Names, characters, businesses, organiza- tions, places, events and incidents either are the product of the author's imagination or are used fictitiously. Any resemblance to actual persons, living or dead, events, or locales is entirely coincidental.

For information contact us at www.boilerplatebooks.com
Book and Cover design by Boilerplate Books, LLC
ISBN: 9780983483588

Print Edition, 2020

10 9 8 7 6 5 4 3 2 1

For my mother

CONTENTS

FOREWARD

It was the late 1980s. A time before email, the World Wide Web, desktop publishing, cell phones, and sadly, spellcheck. Today's LGBTQIA+ was missing more than a few letters and symbols.

I was a 25-year-old lesbian in search of a normal life. It was all I had ever wanted. I did not have a normal childhood or normal parents. We didn't do normal things. I entered the adult world at 19 with *zero* normal. Culturally, the closest I ever came was abnormal. I just couldn't seem to shake those first two letters.

To my government, I was either an outlaw or a political revolutionary. I didn't want my life defined by politics. And for a time, avoided that by diving head-first into the other side of the LGBTQ community: hedonism. It wasn't normal, but it wasn't political.

As a young lesbian in New Hampshire, the only way to find other lesbians without going political was the smoke-filled, unmarked, members-only bars usually found in an abandoned warehouse district.

But private club status did not keep those bars from being raided occasionally by local police, sending a disco-embellished crowd streaming out every exit into the night to avoid capture. And after I lost my second "good" coat from the thrift shop in a raid one November evening, I decided to try politics.

The group, Citizen's Alliance for Gay and Lesbian Rights (aka: CAGLR) in New Hampshire was the first group I joined. They produced a bimonthly newsletter called *Breathing Space*, and it was there that I began a column series called *The Straight and Narrow*.

My goal was to produce a series that was *not* about politics–at least not all of the time. The day was coming when we would have our equality. I was sure it would happen while I was still in my 20s. There had to be more to our lives than politics.

You know, a *normal* life.

But the 1980s were a very political time. The AIDS epidemic coincided with budding, mostly local, forays into LGBTQ equality. The result was panic, fear and violence on a *very* local level. Public opinion was solidly – and loudly – against us.

It's one thing to hear national broadcasters hate you from afar. It's quite another to be constantly bombarded with local politicians, local people on the street, local fear and local hate.

The news for LGBTQ people ran the gamut from bad to terrifying.

And then, like a virus, this mix of fear and politics made its way into – and divided – our community.

The lesbian population in the face of AIDS simply *disappeared*. This created a rift between the L and the G pieces of LGBTQ. Lesbian problems, no matter how bad, couldn't top the AIDS epidemic. Lesbians resented gay men for dragging them into a fresh spotlight of national hatred. Gay men resented lesbians for wasting their time with any other issue but the life-or-death issue of AIDS. Lesbians were in the lowest risk group for AIDS. Gay men? The highest.

Everyone was at a breaking point. Everything about our lives became political. It was unavoidable.

I wanted to try and lighten everyone's load. I wanted to remind the world and lesbians that we were still here, still queer, and still trying to get used to it. We may not have the problems of gay men, but we mattered.

Moving to Maine a couple of years later, I contacted *Our Paper*, the Voice for Gay Men and Lesbians in Maine.

I'm sure the title was meant to establish a sense of *ownership* rather than avoid printing the word GAY or LESBIAN or BI in three-inch-high letters, but what inevitably followed was far worse conversationally:

Me: "I just started working with *Our Paper*."

Friend: "Whose paper?"

Me: "*Our Paper*."

Friend: "My paper? I don't have a paper."

Me: "No, *Our Paper*."

Friend: "Your paper? What paper?"

This could go on for days…

Despite these "who's on first" conversations that followed discussing *Our Paper* with anyone, I continued the series for six years, ultimately becoming the paper's editor and changing the name to the *Gay and Lesbian Times*.

Personal computers arrived midway and my articles were saved on early 8" floppy disks that pre-dated DOS. Desktop publishing followed. We cranked out the paper (almost) monthly despite doing so with a crew of never more than a handful of volunteers. *Our Paper* was mailed statewide—*in a plain brown wrapper*. Even so, some people had *Our Paper* mailed to post office boxes or friends out of state. That's what it was like back then.

Over all those years I attended more than one Gay Pride festival and Gay Pride march. It was very gay, but not very *lesbian*. Portland's Gay Film Festivals always included a dozen gay films of varying degrees of nudity—but only sad, token lesbian flicks. Usually a fully-clothed, black-and-white, sub-titled indie spin on *The Well of Loneliness*—our default lesbian origin story circa 1928. Spoiler alert: it doesn't end happily.

Where were all the fun lesbian stories? You know, the ones where they didn't die. Maybe something less than a hundred years old? In color? I'd settle for *normal*, but was an R rating too much to hope for?

Deep in my own very real closet was a box of back issues of all those *Our Papers*. I had moved them up and down third story apartments to new third story apartments over a quarter of a century, with the hope of compiling them into a book someday. Because, while there were hundreds of books about "Gay Anything" there seemed to be nothing about lesbians.

Gay men showed up in movies and TV shows—subjects of ridicule because they were perceived as "less manly." But lesbians were perceived as a threat to the American ideal of family. You never heard the word, *lesbian*, on TV. In films they were portrayed as witches or predatorial girls' school staff.

Rather than fight us, society just redefined us—or erased us.

But that didn't stop us. From Equal Protection Portland (Maine, 1997) to Marriage Equality (USA, 2013), progress was slow. For every gain? There was a price.

Our *skim milk* relationships became legitimized thanks largely to Supreme Court Justice Ruth Bader Ginsburg. I married my partner after calling the clerk's office to make sure that our special freaking day wouldn't be ruined by an unsympathetic local official. Because victory always came with a side of uncertainty.

Also evolving over time was OCR software and spellcheck. E-publishing was born. In 2015, I dug out that box of back issues and began scanning. All I needed now was a title.

Like many lesbians, I was watching President Barack Obama's State of the Union Address, January 20, 2015, when he said, "I want future generations to know that we are a people who see our differences as a great gift, that we're a people who value the dignity and worth of every citizen — man and woman, young and old, black and white, Latino, Asian, immigrant, Native American, *gay*, straight..."

I looked at my partner. Gay Americans? I mean, Native Americans, Latino Americans… sure. I get it. But Gay Americans? I am not *Lesbian-American*. I didn't *swim* here from the Isle of Lesbos seeking political asylum.

I'm a much more terrifying force to be reckoned with. I'm an American lesbian. I was born here. I pay taxes here.

I don't want my civil rights because I'm a *lesbian*. I want them because I am an *American*.

DROPPING BY AND COMING OUT TO
YOUR GRANDPARENTS

OLD PEOPLE are fragile. Delicate. They don't understand these things. And for those children who get too pushy, *"Don't tell your Grandfather/ Grandmother. It'll kill him/her!"*

In a word: baloney.

I'll grant you that grandparents can be a big challenge, but I can almost guarantee that if it's going to kill anyone it will be *you*.

On my Father's side of the family, my Grandmother was the original southern belle. First one on the hay wagon, ukulele in tune and vocal chords just itching for a rousing chorus of *"I Got a Gal I Do."* Lemonade always chilling in the fridge for any gentlemen callers and a porch swing well-oiled so as not to creak. She worried about me as only a southern grandma can.

What? Pushing eleven and still not interested in boys? She used to enquire in every letter about the status of my dance card and in person would recall her young swains, always assuring me that my attitude problem would radically change. Overnight, perhaps. Just keep reading *Tiger Beat* and everything will be fine.

Overnight? The thought of this wolfman-like transformation horrified me as I saw the day when my individuality would be suddenly but quietly erased. I'd wake up humming "I Got a Gal I Do," toss out my high tops and start squeezing lemons. I already had my own ukulele.

The attempt at imprinting did not work, however, and I found myself living two or three different lives depending on current company. At age fourteen my ulcer was alive and growing. Wanting to tell people who I was and deciding against it because *they* may not be able to handle the news. By the time I had screwed up my courage it was too late to tell my grandmother anything without the help of a Ouija Board.

My Grandfather was the true southern gentleman. In school he majored in martinis with an elective in barbecue. He did not know where anything was in the kitchen, but the lawns were meticulously well groomed. For years our only contact had been the usual birthday card with a crisp ten-dollar bill tucked inside.

As I got older, I made the effort to get to know him. He was set in his ways, but cute as a pin nonetheless. As we corresponded he became more and more interested in my marital plans. What's wrong with all the men up there? (Got a week?) Okay, here goes. I wrote him an honest, though delicate, letter trying to put lesbianism into larger, more bland terminology... mindful of the ever-warned impact this could have.

I sat at home picturing his crumpled body slumped over the mailbox, turning blue... one large vein standing out on his forehead near the left temple... and my opened letter clutched in his hand.

The letter I got *back* was basically "glad to hear you're happy and gay." He didn't get it. Subsequent letters were less delicate, but still did not contain the dangerous word "lesbian." Still no luck. Finally, I wrote a letter with the words "woman" and "sex" in the same sentence. I mailed it, palms sweating and heart pounding.

His answer? Are you a lesbian, dear? Why didn't you just say so? It's okay with me. Whatever makes you happy, sweetheart.

So much for the news killing him. The process had come close to wiping me out.

On my Mother's side of the family? My Finnish Grandmother had only lived in America for 60 years and naturally had never really bothered to pick up the language. I spent a year just learning the Finnish word for "coffee cake" and still had the pronunciation wrong. How would I ever translate lesbian?

Hanna Aiti (Finnish for Grandmother) had always held a special place in my heart. What little I knew of her personal history told me the story of a courageous woman overcoming incredible odds. I wanted to know her and wanted her to know me.

With my Mother acting as interpreter I managed to tell her. Her answer was a shrug and a *"big deal,"* in Finnish, of course. I thought back on the many times I'd been told, "Don't tell your Grandmother!"

Of course, your Grandparents may be a different story. But, if you're interested in telling them the truth, try sitting down and sifting through all the misinformation you've collected over the years. Physical vigor may deteriorate over the years, but mental stability and a sense of *live and let live* seem to increase. Though I didn't write to my Grandparents as often as I should, I can at least share with them my joy of falling in love, fun with friends, work in CAGLR, you name it.

There's nothing drearier than writing an empty, I-am-fine-how-are-you letter. Except receiving one.

650,000 LOST SOULS ON THE
HIGHWAY OF LIFE

OVER THE Columbus Day weekend, I joined about 650-thousand friends in a celebration of courage, identity, and solidarity.

No one noticed.

And I sit here at my word processor, both of us exchanging confused looks. How could nobody notice? Why did nobody notice? I feel like a six-year-old asking why stars occasionally shoot across the sky all of a sudden in one last surge of life, only to die in the darkness without making a sound.

We were really there. I know that much because the pictures came back from the drug store photo desk. There are pictures of people I know and love, pictures of the crowd, couples, protesters, whacko's, everything around me at the time. It was one of the largest marches on Washington in the history of America and nobody noticed.

Every television station dedicated to bringing me the most important, vital news of the day gave the march a 30 to 40 second piece of airtime after ten minutes of in-depth coverage of the football players strike. Every on-the-scene television camera crew shot roughly seven or eight people, who may have been homosexuals, milling around a street corner somewhere and added it to the shots of the religious extremists who were shouting about their concerns for our souls in a manner that biblically allowed them to use words like "homo" and "pervert" and "queer."

Every newspaper dedicated to being the last bastion of truth in a sell-out world estimated the crowd at *100 to 200 thousand*. Well, they were only off by about 450 thousand, but, hey, estimating is not an easy thing to do.

Oh, but just wait till Time magazine comes out! And Newsweek, and Life, and who knows? Maybe even National Geographic! After all, over a million feet stomping all over Washington must have set off some kind of activity in the lower crust of the Earth's surface. A tremor at least. Maybe a small quake.

We waited for the glossy magazine covers showing an aerial view of the teeming millions. Maybe we can blow 'em up on the photocopier and find "us" in the crowd! We waited for congressmen to urgently phone Reagan, demanding his immediate return to Washington. We waited for the National Guard or the FBI to ferret us out and throw us in with other perpetrators of *un-natural acts*. We waited for state legislators to fall to their knees and beg our forgiveness. They had seen the Light. Equality was for everyone.

We expected reactions in the extreme. They would cheer us on—or open fire.

Wheels would start moving. Something, damn it, would happen.

Nobody noticed? Nobody cared? I can't say anything to rationalize it away. The crowd was not big enough to draw attention? The issue was not of any importance? Causes only work during a leap-year?

I had the most incredible three days of my life. That alone is not news worthy, but when half a million people can all say that at the same time and the same place, that is. I carried the New Hampshire banner part of the way to the Capitol! I defaced federal currency with words such as, *"lesbian dinero."* I read, through tears, the names of hundreds of people who had died of AIDS, their names and lives turned into a silent work of quilted art covering the chilly ground.

I walked down a city street for the first time *able to be exactly who I am*. I stood in a crowd of thousands and felt as safe as a I would in my own home. I realized that the sense of freedom I had felt all along was simply a few holes punched into the side of a cage to let in a little sunlight.

I also realized that it would only be a matter of hours before I would have to go back into my cage. I would go back to my job, unable to really tell anyone where I had been. I would go back to my neighborhood where people look at me with suspicion.

I figured the press coverage would be a little off. The TV shots great but not long enough. The magazines in-depth and with the best photos. The society outraged, awakened, motivated, or disgusted.

I just never figured that nobody would notice.

Note:

I wrote this following the Second National March on Washington, October 11, 1987. From Wikipedia:

The 200,000 persons estimate, widely quoted from the New York Times, was made several hours before the march actually began; similarly, most of the pictures the mainstream media used were taken early in the morning, or of the AIDS Quilt viewing area rather than the march itself. Police on the scene estimated numbers during the actual march to be closer to 750,000.

https://en.wikipedia.org/wiki/Second_National_March_on_Washington_for_Lesbian_and_Gay_Rights

IF YOU DON'T LIKE THE WAY I
VOTE...

SOMETIMES VOTING is a right. Other times a responsibility. You notice
how it is never described as anything fun. You don't take your right to
vote out for a pizza and a movie. You "exercise" your right to vote. And
I don't mean bowling, either. Real exercise, the stuff that hurts. Exercise
is one of those things that's "good for you." You know, like bran or taxes.
It isn't fun; it's *endured*.

I look at the current slew of candidates prowling the country, shaking
babies and kissing hands. (Or was that the other way around?) 1988 has
arrived and once again I am being called upon to vote. Years before, I
used to chuckle with the ancient citizens that always seem to be handing
out the little pencils and the big sheets of paper at the various church
basements and Elks lodges that had been converted for the day into
Small Town Polling Place, U.S.A.

Years before, we laughed about the "lesser of the two evils" and
some of the bozos that had come and gone over the past century. Years
before, the faces of Grandma and Grandpa You-Don't-Remember-The-
Depression-But-We-Do, used to positively light up at the sight of such
a young woman at an off-year election, a primary, or even the biggie.

"Not many people your age have a sense of civic responsibility anymore," they'd say.

So, there I was, minding my own business when something went terribly wrong. In the twinkling of an eye I lost my faith in the system. I don't want to vote. I can't find the lesser of the two evils. No matter whom I vote for it will be a mistake. I just KNOW it. Exercising my right to vote? I don't call that exercise. Unless you also refer to a lynching as "jumping rope."

I don't care about Gary Hart and his improprieties. Okay, he had a fling. The press jumped all over it so Gary quit. Then, a clever press agent found a way to use that to Hart's advantage and did. Gary rejoined the battle. To Gary I ask, "Why did you pick such a BIMBO?" Are you just another cuff-link jockey on hormonal overload? Another heterosexual yacht club member who is vacant from the navel on up? I don't think I want to know.

There is a wonderful slew of Democratic hopefuls who are up front about their plans to raise taxes all over the place. As they speak, you can almost hear the sound of a toilet flushing in the background.

Some of the Republican contenders don't have a prayer with me either. I'm not impressed by limited nuclear *anything*. I would rather not have mandatory AIDS testing and am not too big on the idea of concentration camps for the victims. I always thought that victims were the ones you helped and bad guys got punished.

I heard a rumor that George Bush is really an inflatable doll, kept alive by the Society for the Preservation of the Bland. Paul Simon is so nice and innocuous that he MUST be psychotic. I'm afraid to like him. I haven't heard any dirt about him. He seems like he's on the up and up. Why do I have this gnawing fear that if he won the election he would show up at the inauguration wearing a pink tutu and a snorkel? We'd find out that, sure, he's nice and all, but he's nuttier than a pecan pie. Maybe when I see some nude photos I'll breathe a sigh of relief.

So, who am I going to vote for? Simple. I'm voting for Oprah Winfrey for President with Cher as Vice President.

Oh sure, you're thinking that I haven't done my political homework. Not true! I read the entire six-panel biography of Oprah in the funnies of the Sunday edition of the Boston Globe. I've even seen a few of her shows. As for Cher, I've been a loyal fan ever since "Silkwood." I can just picture the two of them together. Oprah would be terrific at handling the Russians. After all, she kept her cool with the residents of all-white Forsythe county. She'd not only know how to ask questions, but she'd even know when the station breaks were due.

Besides, I admire any overweight woman who doesn't take any crap about it.

Cher, on the other hand, has the kind of humor and intelligence that you don't normally find with that kind of body. I would watch anything from a national press conference to the history of the sardine industry if she were in it. The two women have talent in the singing department, they are bright and funny, and damn good looking — what else could America ask for?

What? Still not sold? Well picture this. Soft spotlights sweep the crowd of thousands that showed up for the victory celebration, coming to rest on stage left and stage right. The music kicks in as Oprah Winfrey and Cher enter singing from both sides of the stage.

Oprah: "They say our love won't pay the national debt!"

Cher: "Before it's budgeted, our money's always spent!"

"I guess it's so, we don't have a lot, but at least I'm sure of all the things we got!"

"I got you babe! I got you babe!"

"I got you for the Wall street slump..."

"I got you for atomic dumps!"

"OOPS, I'M SORRY, BUT WE GOTTA BREAK. BACK IN A MOMENT!"

MASTERING THE IRS 10-40 FORM

LIKE MOST lesbians and gay men who have spent another year as illegal aliens in their own country, I look forward to paying taxes. I know it's a sizeable chunk of money when you get a look at your W-2's, but what do you expect? This is a big country and prejudice doesn't grow on trees. It's taught. And that costs money.

Thousands of schools require hundreds of thousands of dollars to enforce and maintain the shining examples of ignorance and terror that have made this country what it is today. Not to mention the money needed to root out homosexual teachers before they go bananas and start accosting fourth graders left and right. They all do, you know. Sure, they may be cool for 20 or 30 years, but sooner or later all that pent-up deviance will explode like a hotdog left in the microwave too long.

Of course, there are the books to think about...It takes time and money to hire all those dogmatic Midwestern grandmothers, outfit them with bifocals and flamethrowers, give them all the list of the 20 or so no-no words/references/allusions and set them loose on the stacks and stacks of revised textbooks and educational materials that come out every year to make sure that only the decent survive. Remember those textbooks you had in school? The ones circa World War I or earlier? They were no accident. They were carefully chosen, hand-picked with spaghetti tongs from the ashes of impropriety. And if they were good enough for William Penn, they are good enough for you.

Do you have any idea just how much it costs to run a newspaper? The newsprint, ink, printing machines? They all have to be maintained. Then throw in the cost of typesetters, layout people, reporters, staffing, and photographers. We're talking big bucks. I know the amount of money I pay in taxes can't support the whole shebang, but every little bit helps in the bigger picture of trickle-down economics. Every time I see a headline like "HOMOSEXUAL ROBBERY," or "HOMOSEXUAL TEACHER FIRED BY PARENTS WHO FEAR AIDS," I know that somewhere my tax dollars are working.

Television time is probably the most influential and definitely the most expensive. Not just the advertising end of it either. All those "Nut 'N Honey" commercials that question the manhood of your average cowboy manage to successfully blend prejudice and salesmanship. The K-Mart ad that suggests a quarterback looks good in a little nightie does the same thing. Many others, however, simply miss out on this golden opportunity.

That's where sitcoms come in. Without that constant level of misinformation generated by every major network, I don't know where we, as a country, would be. Bowing to pressure from the Nielsen families some of the smaller networks and local stations are lending a hand as well. If all else fails, they can fall back on Sunday morning religious programming. In the end the dollar figure is well into the millions, even hundreds of millions. It's worth it, though. With so many two-paycheck households today, parents just don't have the time to instill in their children the generational hatred and fear that are so vital to our country. When I come across a couple of squabbling 10-year-olds in the parking lot of our local grocery store and I hear them hurling comments like, "you faggot," at least I know that they are getting the information somewhere. That somewhere is taxes. It keeps our country running every day.

Lately though I've been hearing rumors that have me a little worried. It seems that one of those dingbat officials in Washington is working on a new tax form called the IRS 10-40 O-NO! Aimed at homosexuals of both orientations, it is a simplified version of the 10-40 EZ form. (Whether you usually use the long form or not.) With the 10-40 O-NO you enter the usual stuff: name, address, social security number, and whether you are filing jointly or singly. You check off the box that has your personal deduction of a thousand bucks or so. This is where it gets a little tricky. Right below that is another line that reads:

I, as a lesbian or gay man request the return of all tax dollars with-held/paid from my annual revenues as a stipulation of living in a country that denies my civil rights, personal freedoms, moral integrity, physical safety, and emotional tranquility.

(Check box to right for full refund)

Assuming that you are gay or lesbian and wish to place a check in the box, your tax dollars in full are returned within the usual waiting period of 10 days, to 3 months.

I don't know about you, but I simply won't stand for it. It's taken me 25 years to get used to this system. I won't have them changing it on me now!

FIRST IMPRESSIONS ARE WRONG
98% OF THE TIME

I WOULD just like to state for the record that I am a girl. A female. A woman. Got it? Everybody in the heterosexual community with me on this one? Any questions? Good.

How many times have you, loyal lesbian readers, been addressed as "sir," "sonny," "young man," "fellow," or "Mr."? It happens to me between three and sixteen times a month, depending on how often I leave the house. You see, these things always happen in public. Now, when I say public I don't mean a couple of people hanging around the express lane in the grocery store. I mean PUBLIC. With a capital "P" that rhymes with "E" and stands for EMBARRASSMENT.

There is no minimum standard for what constitutes a public setting. Like the concept of Yin and Yang, it is a delicate balance. For instance, a small grouping of construction workers can have the same effect as a large group of elderly P.T.A. members. A waiter addressing you as "sir" in the company of your first date can have the same effect as a game show host with an audience of millions.

This problem of gender confusion *("femicus goddamnicus"* in Latin) has dogged my heels for close to twenty-six years and I am beginning to lose my sense of humor about it.

What is it? Is it the mustache? My brother can't grow one to save his soul. I, however, have had one for ten years. I have done everything from bleaching to waxing to weed whipping. Is it the short haircut? I get called "sir" more often as my hair gets longer. Is it the fact that I don't wear dresses? When I have worn dresses in the past, restaurant owners have come up to me and said, "excuse me sir, but if you're going to dress like that. I'm going to have to ask you to leave. We don't want any trouble." I would hate to think that people really know better and are just trying to make my life as humiliating as possible.

The most painful experience takes me back to seventh grade, between chorus and lunch period, on the lawn of the Troy Junior High School. It was there, in the company of close to thirty schoolmates that two little girls approached me. They were giggling and whispering and pointing at me. One of the two, decked out in full little-girl-combat-gear (frilly dress, ribbons in her pony tail, little white socks with the fold-over embroidered edge) ran up to me. Her little bullhorn voice filling the air, "ARE YOU A BOY OR A GIRL?" I froze. Panic swept over me as my eyes darted back and forth over the faces of the bloodthirsty seventh-graders awaiting my answer.

"Why?"

"BECAUSE IF YOU'RE A BOY, MY GIRLFRIEND THINKS YOU'RE CUTE. ARE YOU A BOY?"

"No."

Not only was I not a boy, I had also struck out as a girl as well. The rest of seventh grade is a blank.

Okay, so school is tough on everybody. As an adult I see the world in a different light. Now the best places for gender confusion seem to be restaurants, grocery stores, any mall, gay bars, and the YWCA.

While checking out the Portland YWCA, the nice lady at the pool asked me point-blank, her voice echoing nicely through the pool area as she explained, "the YWCA is for *women*."

The first time I ever went to a gay bar, a gentleman in black leather made a pass at me. I explained that I was not into the whole bondage thing. So much for cruising.

At women's clothing shops in the mall, young women asked me if I am buying something for a friend. When I absent-mindedly say that it's for me, they look horrified or threaten to call the manager. I won't even tell you what happened the time I went into the shop that sold lingerie.

I have managed to cut down on these little encounters by simply shopping by mail, avoiding parties, baby showers, weddings, medical facilities, and dining out. My social life now revolves around natural food stores, car washes, the United States Post Office, and gardening centers. These places seem to score best. The people are friendly and somehow always seem to address me in the female. I also do well with preschoolers and pets.

For the rest of the world, I have developed a simple, mathematical formula for discerning the sex of anyone. It has an accuracy rate of 98%. Here goes:

3 COULD-BE'S ARE GREATER THAN 1 FIRST IMPRESSION

If your first impression of a person is male, but you are not sure, it is a normal response to "could-be". Well, I think it's a boy, but it could be a girl because (#1) he/she has a pony tail, and (#2) is wearing an earring in each ear, and (#3) has a mustache but no beard. As soon as you have mentally accumulated 3 could-be's (2 if they are very strong) they over-rule your first impression. Try it some time. You'll find that it does work. If you are still not sure, simply drop the male or female association from your statement or question until you are sure. That works too.

Like that time at the Holiday Inn. My lover and I had snuck off for a weekend of wild fun and excitement. We were checking into the Holiday Inn and the desk clerk seemed a bit confused. He kept looking me over. No doubt suffering from gender confusion. How did he handle it? Simple. He looked straight at me, then at my partner, and asked her, "Will that be two adults?"

ALLEGED & AVOWED

IT'S NOT easy for me to say this. I am twenty-six years old and have not taken my vows as a homosexual.

As far as the rest of the heterosexual world is concerned, I am still an "alleged lesbian." It's not like I haven't planned to take them. It's just that something last minute always happens, leaving me standing alone at the altar, federal bureau, civil office, or governmental department. How many times I've read headlines about AVOWED HOMOSEXUALS, friends of mine, in the local newspaper. Not to mention my avowed brothers and sisters on a national level, making the news with Dan Rather. Anyone knows that you never really make it big time until you have taken your vows. "Alleged" homosexuals seldom make it any further than local gossip, vicious rumors and passed notes. Take that time back in '78. I was just turning sixteen, had a wicked-intense crush on Kate Jackson, and to prove my undying devotion, was preparing to take my vows as a homosexual. (Back then there were no such things as lesbians.) That was the year that they decided to resurface the floor of the county courthouse for the first time since the Civil War. Next, we got a lot of rain, and to make a long story short, over seventy percent of the available floor space took on the consistency of flypaper. For the next four months, no business short of a murder trial was conducted. Anything of a less serious nature was either postponed or rerouted to the warehouse of Ed's Comfy Couch on route 202.

Then there was the time in 1980 when I was about to take the exam for my Third-Class Radiotelephone Operator's Permit. I figured that while I was in Philadelphia taking the disc jockey exam, I would nip over and get my homosexual vows taken care of at the same time.

I had even gone so far as to get a current copy of the Philadelphia-to-Towanda bus schedule when the law was abruptly changed. No longer was a test even required to become a disc jockey. You simply filled in a post card, mailed it, and the FCC rubber-stamped it. There was no space on the card to declare any sexual preference. The time I got vanity plates for my pick-up, my membership at the YMCA, the free lottery ticket I won in the Tri-State Megabucks, credit card renewals, the list goes on and on. All golden opportunities to take my homosexual vows. All somehow screwed up by fate, bad weather, insufficient postage, or poor memory.

It is for this reason that I suggest that the Trout Pond at L.L. Bean be declared the official site for taking and/or declaring vows based on sexual preference for Maine residents and the unofficial, but still legally valid site for non-resident tourists from across the country. This is with the natural understanding that no sexual harassment, innuendo, or mis-adventure occurs on the part of the L.L. fish residing in said Pond. This does not preclude any state from declaring their own official test site. (New Hampshire might choose *Lechmere's*, or Pat's Peak, for example, and Massachusetts might pick a mutually agreed-upon hot-pretzel vendor along the Boston Commons.) I know what you're thinking, but it's really quite logical. What is the one spot in Maine to which every resident will pay at least one visit before death? The answer is the Trout Pond at L.L. Bean. What is the most fascinating natural attraction at the largest non-governmental body in the state? The answer is the Trout Pond at L.L. Bean. What offers modern-day life in a historic framework? Again, the Trout Pond at L.L. Bean. What is not only fun for the whole family, but a positive and uplifting spiritual experience? What offers the opportunity to come out of the closet in front of several witnesses whose discretion is predetermined? The answer is the Trout Pond at L.L. Bean.

And what has a 100% guarantee of customer satisfaction and a history of excellent service? The answer is L.L. Bean. This is why I suggest the Trout Pond at L.L. Bean and not the Maine Aquarium.

It would be a simple matter for the store to put up a couple of postcard stands on either side of the Trout Pond. The card would allow for individuals to declare their homosexuality or heterosexuality and, at the same time, get on the mailing list for L.L. Bean's latest catalogue. It's quick, easy, and efficient. Even the town has a nice, positive ring to it. Think about it the next time you're in Freeport. And the next time somebody asks if you're gay or straight, tell 'em to "go fish!"

POLITIPHOBIA

ARRRGHH! I sat bolt upright in bed. The clock built into the VCR on the dresser glowed a sleepy 4:15 a.m. My palms were dripping sweat. My heart pounding in my throat. The faint white shadow of my spastic cat, Madigan, zipped past my eyes as he bounded off the bed and dashed for the door. That same dream. Six nights in a row. The election still over a week away.

What did it mean? A figure covered with a sheet, roughly six feet tall, wearing glasses, chasing me through the vacant warehouse section of some large city. In one hand it carried a ballot, in the other a hot-air popcorn popper. A couple of inches of snow had fallen and I was dressed only in a Gay Pride T-shirt, sweat pants, and swim fins. I tried to run, slipping and falling in the slush. The figure chasing me had no problem keeping up. As it ran, it kept waving the ballot and the popcorn popper; screaming, "STAY THE COURSE!"

I was suffering from politiphobia. The gnawing fear that no matter how you cast your presidential ballot you are playing Russian roulette with a fully loaded weapon.

I was beginning to crumble under the strain of trying to find the lesser of the two evils. "Well, I can't vote for Bush, so I guess I'll have to vote for Du... Du...Du..." the word just wouldn't come out. I tried to avoid conversations with Republican friends. I tried to avoid conversations with Democratic friends. I envisioned my Republican co-workers walking slowly toward me, backing me into my office, as they chanted, "Liberal! Liberal! Liberal!" Thank Gosh I found B.A.—Ballots Anonymous.

I didn't say anything at my first few B.A. meetings, I just wanted to take in the atmosphere. Until that Wednesday evening. It was around 7 o'clock. Everyone was getting a cup of coffee and finding a folding chair that would not produce lower back pain. The crowd was a potpourri of differing social and cultural backgrounds. As the meeting got underway, I screwed up my courage to address the group.

"Good evening...my name is Holly and I'm a ...uh, Liberal."

"Good evening, Holly," the group responded.

"I came here tonight because some of my friends think that I need a little help with this election," I lied. "It's not that my mind isn't made up, it's just that I am feeling a little uncertain about my choice. You know, a little guilty. Like, no matter what I do, I'm making a bad decision. I try to weigh the issues logically, but every time I picture myself at the polling place, I feel like I am going to vomit." I managed a weak smile. A few heads nodded in sympathy. "You see, if I vote for George Bush, we'll be thrown into conflict over something like right-of-way laws for the Panama Canal, and the whole planet will end up exploding in a nuclear puff of radioactive debris!" My calm, collected exterior began to give way. My breathing was becoming irregular. My voice climbed an octave. "But I've seen those television ads about Dukakis turning the harbor into toxic Snack Pack, while taxing the middle class of Massachusetts into a life of serfdom! I mean, what the HELL am I supposed to DO?"

I frantically searched the room for answers. Help. Anything.

No one said a word. I felt embarrassed, and with as little ado as possible, quietly took my seat. Part of me felt relief. I had said aloud all those things playing tug-of- war with my conscience. But the other part of me felt as if I had just let out some dreadful family secret – had spoken the unspeakable to a group of total strangers.

I sat quietly in shock for the rest of the evening.

The group wrapped-up a little after 9 o'clock with a few deep breathing exercises and positive visualization. We each received a bro-chure filled with "voting day stress tips" along with the 1-800 number of a toll-free hotline set up just for this election. We were supposed to dial 1-800-CAN-VOTE if we felt dizzy or short-of-breath on Election Day. A team of volunteers would take us to the polls and talk us through the whole thing.

I had put on my jacket and started for the door when a young man approached me. "Don't worry," he said, "The first meeting is always the toughest."

"Yeah. Next week will be better."

"Well, I'm off to see some friends. How about you?"

"Oh, I think I'll go home and make some popcorn and watch the news on CNN," I smiled. "You know, the usual."

HOW SENSUAL AM I?

THERE IT was again. That same dream. I glanced at the VCR for the time. It read 4:15 a.m. A white shadow of a cat slowly crept up to me in the dark, plopped into my lap, and let out a sigh between the blankets.

Monday, Wednesday, and now, Thursday night, the same story played over and over in my mind as I slept. In the dream I am running through the women's section of Filene's wearing nothing but an old pair of sweats. I am being chased by a SWAT team of Avon ladies armed with everything from eyebrow tweezers to leg make-up. My mind confused by all the strangely angled mirrors, I take a wrong turn and find myself running up the down escalator. The yelping bark of pit bulls gets louder and louder. I run faster, but I can make no headway. Exhausted, I collapse against the metal stairs that slowly escort me back to my doom. Several manicured hands grab for my arms and legs. I hear laughter. Menacing laughter.

And then I wake up.

It's not easy to be a lesbian in today's world. You plan an evening out with a special someone. You get dressed in your Saturday night best. Even you have to admit that you are hot stuff. Looking good! But as you walk into the restaurant you notice certain differences. The other women have given a totally different definition of "hot stuff." Decked out in slinky, off-the-shoulder numbers, spiked heels, and make-up expertly applied, they and their escorts look at you with curiosity mixed with just a pinch of aggression.

The aggression I'm used to. It's the curiosity that hurts.

You stand there, feeling beads of sweat forming on your upper lip. You wonder: Is my fly unzipped? My shirt sticking out? Cat fur on my suit? A quick trip to the ladies' room reveals that everything is in place. You straighten your tie and return to the dining room. So, what's the problem?

Why do they seem to be looking at you or–worse yet–trying to stifle a giggle. You know that if you were at the local women's bar you would see a dozen mirror images of yourself.

It's a real confidence-basher and it's all around us. Every damn day.

Last month I took the quiz in Cosmopolitan magazine called "How Sensual Are You?" It was on page 136, tucked between hundreds of ads featuring glamorous and glitzy women, oozing sex appeal; and articles covering every vital topic for today's women: Marrying Down [Would You Be Up to It?]; What Fantasies Can Do for You; How to Give Yourself A Professional Manicure; even a chat with Oliver North! Looking over the quiz, my partner and I did the usual editing of changing all the male references to female. This time, however, I found that was not enough. In fact, I ended up with a score of average ONLY after stretching the truth to the very breaking point. Half the questions I couldn't REALLY answer at all.

For example:

1. The first thing I do in the morning is:
    a. Read the newspaper.
    b. Eat breakfast. Café au lait and a hot, buttery croissant with sweet jam make me feel pampered and sophisticated.
    c. Take long shower-first very hot, then icy cold to get my blood racing.
    d. Nothing. I like to stretch out between the sheets for a while.

What? Where does feed the cats, jump in the shower, sprinkle-food the goldfish, gobble a bowl of raisin bran and dash to work fit in? Or how about:

14. One of the most important things at work, other than the job itself is:

    a. Male co-workers I can flirt with just a little.

    b. A pleasant environment-good chair, attractive desk, decent light.

    c. A window. I want to see interesting things outside.

    d. Good restaurants near the office.

Flirt with my co-workers? You must be joking! A pretty desk? Nice restaurants? How about: E. A paycheck that I can actually live on.

You've already heard what happens in restaurants. Many questions didn't seem to apply one way or the other. For example: [true or false] 4. My girlfriends laugh at my compulsion to buy luxurious lingerie. Well...

I browse through the magazine positively spellbound. I turn to my partner and say, "Gosh, I wonder what it's like to be a woman...you known, *a real woman.*" Reading magazines, watching television, I feel a creeping sense of sexual limbo. I certainly don't qualify as a man. But if the female images all around me are the standard, then I don't come that close to being a woman either.

Where are the gorgeous lesbians on TV, in magazines, or movies?

I know it takes time. But women have these things called "primes," you know. And if the country doesn't make some changes real soon, I could hit mine and be on the downhill side... my prime only visible in the rear-view mirror.

TRACKING THE WILD LESBIAN

I DON'T remember a time when there weren't lesbians, but my grand-mother does. There weren't any lesbians when she was a young woman growing up in THE SOUTH. The world was still a decent place to live. There were gentlemen and there were ladies. Women did not pump their own gasoline. Ever. Oh, sure, you occasionally found a nice young man who seemed hesitant in the face of marriage, but with enough pressure "gently applied" by every living relative, clergyman, and employer, they almost always came around. If they flatly refused? They went North.

However, there were *no lesbians*. **None.** (Of course, I am translating here, as my own grandmother would have never used such a word.)

So where did lesbians come from? Naturally my grandmother did not want to even think about that. All she knew is that IF there even were "those type of women" they certainly came from the North and they probably were the result of marrying Northerners. (This was said with all the affection that a cotton-picker would have for boll weevils.)

The first problem in tracing the roots of HOMOSEXUALITY is the word. You just can't go around saying "sex" to a woman in her late 70s without getting into trouble. I don't care how detached and his-torical you think you are being. I can almost guarantee that you'll be outshouted, tackled, and gagged by friends and family before you even get past "homo." Also, saying "sex" in a country founded by Puritans is an open invitation to be roasted slowly over hot coals as soon as you return from the talk show circuit.

So how about changing the words? *Homo*genderous and *Hetero*genderous sound a lot nicer. I think they even add greater depth to the terms.

Sexuality means: *The condition of having sex; sexual activity; or expressive of sexual receptivity or interest especially when excessive.*

Excessive? Thanks a lot, Merriam Webster. Remind me to have 40 cheese pizzas delivered to your house at 3 a.m.!

Gender, on the other hand, means: the state of being male or female (typically used with reference to social and cultural differences rather than biological ones). It's not a lot better, but at least it gets rid of the "s" word.

"Gay" and "lesbian" are also a problem. "Gay" lacks any sense of seriousness. It's also kind of cute. When shouting for gay rights at rallies, I have found myself privately wishing for a slightly heavier-duty word. Something with more weight.

"Lesbian" is—for reasons completely unknown to me—too *exotic* for your average American. In telling people that I am a "lesbian" I have received replies like, "oh, really? I'm a protestant," "I've always wanted to learn how to do that, did you take a class?" or my favorite, "have you lost any weight yet?"

The second problem with tracing our roots is the flat denial of people to even admit that we exist.

When you think about it, it's a damn clever move. This way we spend our whole lives wrapped up in an idiotic, existential argument. Just imagine George Bush campaigning on the ticket that Democrats don't exist. The Democrats would be so nonplussed that they'd never get themselves organized enough to pick a candidate.

Many gays and lesbians go through tons of soul searching, questioning, and half a dozen therapists before they can even bring themselves to declare their lifestyles. Only to be told that there are *no homosexuals.*

The only answer I can see is to fight *willful invisibility* with super-visibility. From now on, as far as I'm concerned, famous gays and lesbians include anyone who has not *publicly declared heterosexual status.* Allowing the gay/lesbian community to lay claim to everyone from queen Nefertiti to George Armstrong Custer. And we won't stop there… Santa Claus, Super Man, Ferris Bueller. I always thought Tarzan was gay anyway. And as for Jane? Any woman who swings on a vine and likes animals gets my vote.

PENNSYLVANIA BURNING

I HAVE never been to one of my class reunions. I don't even know if the class of 1980 from Troy Senior High has even had a class reunion yet. If they have, I never heard about it...and I graduated Valedictorian. You'd think I would have received an invitation.

When I left Troy, Pennsylvania–home of the Troy Trojans (Yeah, yeah — I know. No jokes, please.) There was something like $13.47 in the class war chest. I know this because I remember hanging around the gym with the other 196 members of my graduating class, practicing cadence and other graduation aerobics, when we were called together for a lecture from one of the faculty members.

She opened by reminiscing over the good old days when students took some pride in their school, unlike our class. She then told us that we were the first graduating class in Pennsylvania history to have coughed up so little money for our class treasury, and that this was a good indication of the type of disorganized, pathetic, shabby futures we could expect for ourselves.

She also tossed in a couple of tidbits regarding how disappointed she was with us and that marking her words, the day would come when we would realize that she was right all along and we had wasted the best years of our lives. She closed by waving a fistful of crumpled dollars in one hand while exposing a handful of loose change in the other, and then, with an explosive sigh, walked out.

I never saw her again.

High school was not the best years of my life. It ranks among some of the worst. Most teenagers will tell you the same thing. In our school, you had three options: fit in with the "in" crowd, be on the outer fringes of the "in" crowd, or fit in with the group affectionately known as the "*scuz*."

As a young lesbian going through that typical stage of paranoid schizophrenia around puberty, I did not fit in with the "in" crowd. I did not have a 1) boyfriend, 2) school jacket with pins, 3) class ring. I never attended dances, sporting events, plays, proms, anything.

I revolved around the outer fringes of the semi-in crowd. I had a 4.0 average, so many students relied on me to help them through Spanish, Chemistry, English, you name it. I also had a somewhat caustic sense of humor that was just vicious enough to drive teachers crazy, but not enough to get me expelled.

This broke up the monotony of some classes. But, overall, I was very much a loner. If it hadn't been for spending those rainy afternoon study halls in the school cafeteria–with its horrible bright orange design–sipping my trademark 7-up and playing cards with this wonderful woman a year older than myself, I don't know what I would have done. She had long brown hair, shy blue eyes hidden behind glasses, a lovely smile, and always wore a navy-blue pea coat...the kind with the little anchors on the buttons.

Those daydreams I used to have of us? Living together in a log cabin in the Yukon where she could practice her flute and I could cartoon, undisturbed by the intrusion of modern society? I kept those dreams to myself. Looking back on them now I find myself smiling a lot and blushing a little.

I don't know whatever became of the class of 1980. A bunch of them got married, a couple got killed, and the rest of them are probably growing into their parents. I look through the old yearbook at least once a year as I am cleaning my art studio and get sidetracked. I try to pick out those students who may have turned out to be gay or lesbian.

There's no real way to know.

In a town the size of Troy, where I went to school, it's not the kind of thing that is seen as proper to be, to discuss, or even to think about.

I picture my partner and I, dressed to the nines, walking into the Commons Building (the name given the new gymnasium built in 1978). The music stops, the whites of eyes become visible even in the darkness, an audible gasp escapes the crowd, and somewhere behind the stacks of old Bee Gees 45s, a flaming torch appears...and then another...and another. A pack of bloodhounds come snarling and barking from behind the buffet table that holds the $13.47 worth of Cheez-Its, bologna-wraps, and olives-run-through-with-those-tiny-plastic-swords.

Paranoid? Probably. But I got to tell you, this July, my partner did go to her class reunion. Not only was it her 20th class reunion (a biggie), but it was held in her hometown in this state! Maine! Not only that, but she took me with her.

We walked into the dining hall filled with couples. She introduced me to some old classmates, had dinner, and even survived the children's photo segment of the evening. Nobody was nasty. Nobody was violent. And nobody asked us to leave. Some folks were not as polite as others, but a few people made up for that by voluntarily–and visibly–chatting me up.

It took a lot of courage for my partner to do that. The lesbian equivalent of "the right stuff." I don't know if I would have the same guts. But I guess I'll get my opportunity in the year 2000, when my 20th reunion comes up. All I can say is, "lookout, Pennsylvania..."

THE ONLY THING WE HAVE TO FEAR
IS ... LESBIANS?

MAYBE IT's just me, but the thought of being incarcerated in a prison cell the size of a bus station bathroom with Zsa Zsa Gabor fills me with a terror that I cannot even begin to describe. That voice...all that make-up...those clothes. UGH!

In glancing through the local newspaper, I saw an article about Zsa Zsa Gabor. It seems she is in a squabble with the police over being pulled over with out-of-date registration stickers, only to find an open bottle of consumable alcoholic substance in her vehicle. She is now trying to plea-bargain her way out of prison on the grounds that she is afraid of *all the lesbians in prison.*

The sadness in this whole incident is that people like Zsa Zsa Gabor have little claim to fame now. Heavenly bodies downgraded to meteorites sprinkled among the stars of Beverly Hills. They burned brightly for a few moments, fizzled and died. The rest of their lives spent looking heavenward in the night sky saying, "Look! I was there...once."

However, the quick cure for a lack of fame is simple. Infamy. Grab some headlines with some outrageous behavior. Claim to be pregnant with the baby of Elvis. Drive your Camaro into the swimming pool of Dr. Joyce Brothers.

In the case of Zsa Zsa Gabor, the supposed quintessential female of her day, despoil that image of femininity with the obscenity of lesbianism.

After all, if Zsa Zsa is the "ideal" in womanhood, then lesbians must be the antithesis.

I do not wish a prison sentence upon this aging woman. A woman dependent enough upon alcohol to have an open bottle of hooch in her car. Instead, I think twenty or thirty hours of community service within the gay community might be enough. Working phone lines, information tables, what-have-you, at a few GAY PRIDE rallies.

In the event that she gets sent up the river, however, I have put together a list of ways for her to identify lesbians. This list is by no means complete, but it is a few likes and dislikes for her to go by.

What do Lesbians Like?
_ Movies
_ Chocolate
_ Going Dancing
_ Long Walks
_ Going Barefoot
_ Having Friends Over
_ Springtime
_ Drives in the Country
_ Garage Sales
_ Planting Gardens
_ Fried Dough
_ Going to the Beach
_ Household Pets
_ Flowers
_ Autumn
_ Renting Videos
_ Visiting Friends
_ Bowling
_ Skiing
_ Lobster

_ The First Snowfall
_ Swimming
_ Reading
_ Going to the Park
_ The Holidays
_ Cooking
_ Children
_ Miniature Golf
_ Looking for Antiques
_ Summertime Country Fairs
_ Sailing
_ Sleeping Late on Weekends
_ Going out on Dates
_ Picking-your-own-apples
_ Good Books
_ Art Museums
_ Christmas Cards
_ Hanging Out
_ Making Snowwomen
_ New Cars
_ Broken-in Jeans
_ Racquetball or Tennis
_ Getting the Christmas Tree
_ Doing Nothing
_ Legos

What Do Lesbians Hate?

_ Intolerance
_ Getting Up Early
_ Traffic Jams
_ PMS
_ Looking for a Parking Place

_ Stereotypes
_ Government Forms
_ Ignorance
_ Renting videos that turn out to be Lousy
_ Misunderstanding
_ Working Late
_ Paper Cuts
_ Taxes
_ Cleaning the House
_ Car Problems
_ Prejudice
_ The Flu
_ Stubbing Toes

You see, when it comes right down to it, we're a pretty common bunch. I would even say that we're ALMOST like everybody else. I tossed in the "almost" because I think, in general, gay men and lesbians have a little "something extra".

Sometimes I wonder how long your average heterosexual could stand up under the pressure of being treated like a criminal by society at large. How long could he or she, if married, stand to be ignored by insurance companies, families, and employers. Refused justice by an openly intolerant society on almost any legal issue. Treated with contempt by religious groups. Assumed to be mentally or emotionally deranged by a society that will then turn around and not really try too hard to prosecute anyone who just killed someone coming out of a gay bar.

I can hear it now, "well, when you put it THAT WAY, of course it sounds bad. BUT...".

Considering how well Zsa Zsa stood up to the pressure of being stopped for expired registration stickers, I can't imagine her holding up well under the daily pressures that face almost every gay and lesbian individual in this country.

Not only that, *Dahlink*, but I don't know where she's ever going to find a prison-striped mink coat.

DENIALITIS

JOB INTERVIEWS are not only the most stress-provoking experience a person can undergo, short of an I.R.S. tax audit or laser surgery, but they provide perfect examples of "denialitis' — [Noun] [pron: dee-ny- *ulil*-i-tiss] an experience of physical/emotional hazard unique to gays and lesbians: causing confusion, frustration, depression, headaches, upset stomach, clammy-hands, and profuse sweating.

It is the resulting symptomatology experienced when an honest person feels forced to lie.

My partner and I recently celebrated our three-year anniversary. I love her more today than ever. I have an enormous amount of respect for the work that she does. Every fiber of my being is–in some way–a reflection of her influence upon me, mixed with a ton of my own neurosis.

I don't want to hide the fact that I share my life with this woman. You see: mentally, spiritually, and emotionally she makes me happy. It shows. It slips out. I can't help it.

I give every potential employer a copy of my resume. I don't get a copy of *theirs*.

I don't know if they are gay or straight, members of Green Peace or the Ku Klux Klan. Conservative or Liberal, Catholic or Hindu.

I naturally wish to seem as friendly and normal as possible. I don't want to say or do anything that makes them think I am unstable. Weird, or "trouble." I usually try to project the image of a Girl Scout with a good sense of humor.

So, what do I do when they start asking those little personal questions?

EXAMPLE: "Does your husband work around the Portland area?"

OPTION 1: STATE YOUR RIGHTS

"I'm not married and please refrain from asking non-job-related questions, or pursuant to subchapter 13, paragraph 34 of the penal code. I will be forced to sue."

This is always a real winner with a potential boss. Scratch that.

OPTION 2: A SHORT LIE

"I'm not married." This, followed by a noncommittal, wan smile may get you out of trouble. But, usually it leads to further troubles: (A.) Not wishing to get yourself tangled in a web of lies about groups and activities that sound wholesome, but to which you do not belong, you opt for the answers that imply that you do nothing in your free time but talk to your hydrangea, study rug-hooking, and read.

This makes most employers assume that you are either a shut-in or emotionally unhealthy—a recluse. *Scratch that.*

(B.) Not wishing to sound like a shut-in. you imply that your free time is spent dancing the night away at singles' bars, meeting interesting and fun people on white-water rafting trips, and learning how to make sushi.

This makes most employers assume that you're a bit unstable. Haven't settled down. You could be unreliable. *Scratch that.*

OPTION 3: A LONG LIE

"I'm not married. After my husband. Steve, a noted archeologist, was killed in a pyramid accident that was the result of an ancient booby-trap dating back to the time of King Tut, I have never considered remarrying. And never will. No one could ever replace him."

This, assuming your potential employer is not an historian, just makes you look like you're babbling, like your whole life is an open book, and maybe you couldn't be trusted with company secrets. *Scratch that.*

OPTION 4: THE TRUTH — VARIETY A:

"My ＿＿ is the Executive Director of a nonprofit agency."

Editorial note: there is no good word to put here:

    a. Partner–too business like, they won't get it.

    b. Significant Other–too stupid.

    c. Lover–too personal.

    d. Wife–forget it. Ditto for husband.

    e. Mate–sounds like Clan of the Cave Bear

    f. Girlfriend–see "Wife".

    g. Roommate–this never works.

    h. The woman I live with–sounds like a spinster aunt.

    i. "name"–using your partner's name will work, but you must see THE TRUTH–VARIETY B

OPTION 4: THE TRUTH — VARIETY B:

"[Name] is the [Job Title]. We have been together for 3 years and are in the process of remodeling a lovely house on [Street Name] in [City]. We are like any other old married couple. We have fun on the weekends, take drives in the country or rent videos. We have a couple of cats and two goldfish."

I hate to say it. but I have yet to come across an employer who didn't look completely stunned by this response.

I usually opt for option 2.

I know I have an active imagination, but no matter how many times I promise myself to just lay it on the line, I still find myself worrying that the word "lesbian" will be nothing but a faint echo from my lips, lost amid the sounds of me screaming and the thrashing of hungry alligators in a blood-filled pool beneath the trap door concealed by a throw-rug in front of the boss' desk.

The chair, a coffee cup. and my resume plummet out of sight as a squeaky hinge snaps shut, and my potential employer whispers into the intercom, *"Miss Brewster, please send in the next candidate."*

But option 2 always leaves me with a queasy feeling. The feeling that I have just done an injustice to myself. If I get the job. I want to punch the employer right in the nose for putting me through such an ordeal. If I don't get the job. I want to do the same thing for putting me through such an ordeal—*for nothing.*

Instead, I usually opt for option 2. Smile and say nothing.

I always hate myself later.

IMAGE FOR SALE—SLIGHTLY USED

No DOUBT about it. The 1990's are the best time in recorded history to be a lesbian. No matter what. True, we don't legally exist, and must occasionally conceal our lives from family members or co-workers, but, hey, we are no longer driven from our villages by packs of bloodthirsty Dobermans.

Despite all this, it's a great time to be a lesbian. I feel a great sense of personal freedom and "general" acceptance from the outside world, and "genuine" acceptance from about 67% of the people I know.

The problem? I just don't know who they are accepting.

It's a hard, life-long task for any of us to chisel out a definition of ourselves from the stone face of society. Tradition is a key factor. Tradition is the safely net of society.

As we cling to the mountain side, not knowing what to do or where to go, we can always ask, *"What did my parents do when this happened to them?"* We count on the safety net of society for clues to behavior, values, and ideas. But what happens to those who are denied by society? Those for whom the safety net is much smaller. I don't have a great grandmother who was also a lesbian and *faced a similar situation* — at least to my knowledge.

I never sat down with any friends or parents, and gained advice about how Debbie was not good enough for me, or how Ms. Right would come along when the time was right. I never heard radio songs about how two women fell in love or saw movies of teenage girls in love — *with each other*. I never had those early dates where mom and dad would let you borrow the car with the understanding that you and Kat would have it home by 11:00 p.m.

So where is my safety net? My tradition? As a lesbian trying to carve out my mountain side, it seems like I was given the wrong tools. Or no tools. It has left me with a sagging sense of identity.

As the pendulum swings between self-denial and active political protest, it ends up coming to rest somewhere in the middle. A place where nothing was before. A place where I must start from scratch. What do I do? People have advised me for years to just "be myself." Of course, they also gave that advice to *Sybil*, and we know how that turned out.

I was the first girl in the history of Croman Elementary School to wear pants to school. Troy, Pennsylvania, was almost turned upside down by a seven-year-old girl in second grade who refused to wear dresses. My mother got calls from the school. Little girls in the playground humiliated me with a non-stop barrage of taunts about being a boy. Others humiliated me even more by telling me that if we were too poor, their mothers would buy me a dress. All of this because I liked to climb on the jungle gym and couldn't with a dress on since the boys crowded under the jungle gym just for the view.

Presto! My first image was born. RADICAL. And it followed me for ten years. I can't help but wonder how different my life would have been if I had just worn the damn dress. I still think about it when I see a jungle gym.

As a teenager in high school, I went through the usual anguish of wanting desperately to be pretty, to fit in, to be liked — as I was none of the above, really. I had this creeping sense of doom — that I wasn't "normal" and that if I was smart, I would never mention *my schoolgirl crushes* to another living soul.

As my girl *friends* began to gather *boyfriends*, I found myself alone. Shut-out from the so-called "best years of your life." Somewhere in there my next image was born. SCHOOL CYNIC. I was the smart kid with the cynical sense of humor.

My classmates wanted someone who could outsmart the teachers, and thereby, relieve the boredom of school. I took on the job, if for no other reasons than to ditch my earlier image. Privately, I was as miserable as any early teen. The difference is that I couldn't talk about it. I couldn't talk about how cute so-and-so was, or how my heart was breaking.

In rural Pennsylvania circa late 1970s that's the stuff of locker room murders. At least in a small farming town. Instead, I tried to forget any sick ideas I had and jump back into the mainstream.

I figured I could be the perfect girl if I really set my mind to it. My target was the sophomore hop. My mother had very generously helped me pick out and pay for a pretty dress for the event. I had told everyone in advance that I would be wearing a dress, hoping that they would have enough time to *extract their pound of flesh before the actual event*. Holly in a dress? News traveled fast.

When I arrived, classmates gathered like sharks detecting blood in the water and let me have it. I kept my dignity. I tried to laugh it off. I also left about fifteen minutes after I arrived, hanging around in a parking lot for an hour or so until my mother was scheduled to pick me up.

I never attended another school event.

Where were all those lesbian juniors and seniors? Sisters or aunts? Where was my safety net? It wasn't there.

Going into my junior year, I went on a diet and lost 35 pounds of pre-teen weight, grew my hair longer, added highlights, and made every attempt I could to look like Farrah Fawcett. Just to impress those boys around whom I wished to spend no time.

I returned to school in my image of the perfect girl. I was smart, funny, and I was actually kind of pretty. I thought it would be everything it was cracked up to be.

To my surprise, none of my friends or classmates noticed the brand new me. I had tried so hard—for nothing. It all seemed like such an act.

Was it this way for everybody? I had no way of knowing.

I slipped through the cracks into despair and depression, becoming the SCHOOL HERMIT. I avoided people, went on binges where I wouldn't eat for days, became suicidal, and seldom talked to anyone.

I didn't have any close lesbian friends, lesbian teachers, anyone to turn to. Half way through the year I almost fainted in the hallway between classes. I hadn't eaten in four days. A girl a year older, a senior noticed. She helped me to the stairs so I could sit down. When she asked what was wrong, I told her I was invisible.

After graduation I became a disc jockey. That image was the INVISIBLE VOICE.

I worked nights, days, sign-ons, and sign-offs. No one ever saw me there, either. I just couldn't find a place within myself where I felt I had a right to exist. And as a disembodied *voice*, no one would be able to track me down.

Despite my Garbo-like existence, I made a friend who also worked nights. He was responsible for me ever having seen the inside of a gay or lesbian bar. I was amazed to see other gays and lesbians, but it scared me that the places where we found them were often these ramshackle underground bars, off in a warehouse district somewhere. Some of them were homes for alcoholics. Others, drug addicts.

I remember one "women's bar" where I was denied access (because I was with a man.) The glimpse I got, through the chain-lock on the door was of several women lined up at a dingy, poorly-lit bar, sitting about three feet apart, steadily drinking.

They didn't even seem to be talking. This was my safety net?

I had come to the end of the journey to find this? I decided that, if this was the *net*, I would aim for the *holes*. I spent a good year of my life getting drunk in bars like that. Until one night at a regular watering hole I found myself thinking, "what losers. I see them here every night..." It was my last night out.

I left radio, lured by the attraction of stepping up to minimum wage, daylight hours, and a non-alcoholic diet. I wanted to see what it was like for normal people who worked at a *desk*…in a *company*… and maybe had a *salad* every now and again.

I ended up moving to Maine, where I am now the MIDDLE-CLASS LESBIAN. Steady relationship, two cats, two goldfish, steady job, finishing up my college degree in computer science. I alternately love and hate my life.

Ultimately, there may not be a safety net for me. Or maybe we all have to learn to weave our own, using the past as thread.

I hope to see a time during my life when a young lesbian in high school can be just as miserable and heartbroken as any other teenager. Not because she feels alone as a lesbian, but because *Ms. Right* turned out to be *Ms. Forget-it*.

STARTING FROM SCRATCH – SOME
ASSEMBLY REQUIRED

I RECENTLY watched the P.O.V. [Point Of View] Documentary series concerning a man's transsexual journey to womanhood. Women through-out the hour-long production responded in a variety of ways. Some could not believe this man was serious. Others seemed to think it was about time. Still others noticed how this man was attempting to take on all the female stereotypical traits that they had been struggling to rid themselves of for years. How to balance vulnerability with independence. How to be self-sustaining yet nurturing. How to appear feminine while using societal standards that are, on one hand, obsolete yet, on the other hand, unquestioned.

Unquestioned.

How long would high heels remain in fashion if men wore them? Leg irons are more comfortable. Most women's clothing is restrictive. Once you decide to wear a skirt and heels, you have to relearn all the basics. Walking, stairs, bending, getting in and out of cars, and picking things up off the floor. Anything less than a $20 bill? It may not be worth it. Everyone knows how ridiculous this is and yet no one says a word. Why? It's unquestioned.

As we watched the transformation of "Garry" into "Gabi," the announcer explained the condition occurring when individuals identify with the opposite gender. These individuals cannot live in peace with themselves; yet offer themselves up as prime targets for bible-thumping fundamentalists, close-minded families or friends, and unsympathetic employers if they attempt to alter their lives by altering their bodies. Why the hatred? Don't we all suffer from a little gender dysphoria?

One of my goals for this year was to try and decide whether or not I wanted to be a woman, and what that meant.

In this society men lead better lives. They often have better jobs and make more money, thanks to archaic assumptions that men bring home the paychecks that support entire families.

Men are sexually unencumbered by the realities of pregnancy. I'm sure there are men who would say this is unfair. That they are very responsible. To those six men I apologize. But let's face facts. Men are still raised and reassured from all sides that sex equals fun. Women never get this message despite typically being there when men are having that fun. And if you're a woman who likes sex? Oh, God.

To even a casual observer, being a woman meant coming in second. Always. For this I was supposed to be happy?

During twelve years of public school it was not unusual to be told that girls didn't have the mind for math or history or anything heavier than home-ec. That my career options were limited to stewardess, secretary, English teacher, or mom. That girls were too weak for sports. That I should try harder to be pretty or no one would "want" me —or, my favorite, "take" me. Which I guess is what happens when "want" is no longer on the table.

The average female ego is wrapped in ever-tighter bonds from day one. A psychological form of cultural foot binding. Church, school, parents, family, everyone crushing that ego into a smaller, twisted space year by year until it can barely stand on its own when it reaches maturity. It's intentional. And it's unquestioned.

As a lesbian, however, my ego constantly rebelled. Forever unwrapping those cultural bindings to the frustration and disdain of all around me. Like a homeless child living on the streets my ego was untrained and malnourished and ultimately, ignored by society.

My mother and I have always been best of friends. One evening, however, we got into one of those discussions that followed a public television special on "homosexuality." We both felt that the majority of humankind, unencumbered by societal pressures, would find themselves to be more bisexual, though most people would probably focus on one gender or the other.

I made the mistake of saying, "well, if I had to choose, the choice would be obvious."

"And that choice would be?" she asked with a smile.

"Well, *women*," I said.

The word had come out of my mouth in the form of dry whisper. Quick as a bolt of lightning. As if I had just confessed to killing someone.

"So, you're telling me you're a LESBIAN?" my mother asked.

"Uh, yeah."

I couldn't even say the word. Worse yet, I had forced my mother to say the "L" word. Out loud. Inside I was cringing, waiting for the hand of God to blow me apart with a plague of locusts, or a one-way ticket to Hell. My heart was pounding, I was sweating, my eyes were darting around the room, avoiding my mother's gaze.

"That's a very interesting decision," she said. And that was the end of the discussion.

I was twenty years old. I'll never forget that sense of terror. All because I told my mother a little bit about myself.

Of course, she didn't say anything positive about it, either. It was an "interesting decision." That covers a lot of ground. Hi-jacking airplanes is also an interesting decision. Was is supportive? It didn't sound all that supportive...

And what next? Was I even a lesbian? Was I sure? Because I just confessed to being a lesbian. In front of my mother. In rural Pennsylvania. Couldn't take that back. I'd never even been on a date.

Women are not genetically second-class citizens. So, I have no problem with being a woman. I do have a problem with cultural prejudice masquerading as tradition. We are born into a cultural passion play of lies, hatred, and fear. Or as the new lingo of the 90's would put it; misdirected information, individual differentiated viewpoints, and basic reactionary urges. We are taught to treat with fear and distrust anyone straying from the accepted majority view for the sake of the herd.

The herd provides the perception of safety and discourages people from leading or thinking for themselves too much. We herd women into a large cultural pen, then surround the lesbians and divide the herd. We tell both groups that they are bad and that the smaller group threatens the safety of the larger. We don't question the herd for fear of becoming a target. I get it.

What I don't get is why we choose to maintain the status quo once we are in a position to dismantle it. When things go unquestioned for too long we lose our ability to question them.

Growing up in farm country I never once met a pregnant woman who ever confessed that she was "hoping for a girl." The best I got was "hoping for a boy, but would take *anything* as long as it was healthy." Anything? That's how we women define ourselves? You're either a man or–anything?

I am a woman. And a lesbian. I may not fit in with heterosexual women or even lesbians, really. Not everyone fits in. We are all individuals. We only look like a herd from a distance. Defining yourself as an individual is more important. Who was I?

I decided to write a personal ad. Personal ads are like a cultural version of an elevator speech. What are your positive traits? How would you describe yourself to others in a positive way? How would you try to reach out to the herd while being an individual? It's not as easy as it sounds. My first attempt came out like:

SWL –27 years old. Good sense of humor. Looking for woman who can take a joke.

It didn't sound all that positive.

Maybe a different approach. The August copy of Food & Wine magazine rated wines and beers. Did I consider myself to be a dry and distinguished Gewürztraminer? Or a bright, appetite-whetting Sauvignon Blanc? How about Chardonnay: consistently outstanding, long, lingering, and complex. Zinfandel's lush, fruity, and wonderfully-drinkable? For wines they all seemed just a bit too intimate.

I switched to beers. Category one was for the light-bodied, dry, crisp and simple. Next came light-to-medium with a touch of sweetness. Then dry, winy, with some bitterness. Finally, heavy and fairly bitter. This seemed closer to reality.

I decided that, for the moment, I would be a Rolling Rock. And came up with this:

SWL–27; good sense of humor. Superb when the occasion calls for simple, light refreshment. Goes great with hot or spicy foods.

ANTS ON THE SIDEWALK

SUMMERS IN Maine are different from the summers of my childhood in Pennsylvania. Pennsylvania summers were hot and dry and long. Fields of timothy hay ringing with the sounds of grasshoppers. Overgrown blackberry brambles that challenged the very brave with dark, sweet berries covered with the tiniest peach fuzz. Brown-eyed Susans and chicory that over-took over any untended land. Dirt roads that kicked up a golden cloud of dust, a mile long, behind any motorist.

Summer started in late May or early June and ended at the end of September. I didn't know anyone who owned a boat. I don't remember seeing even one tourist in all those years.

Summers in Maine are beautiful in a different way. They seem to bloom just at the point when the rest of the country has gone to summer's seed. Just as phone calls of record highs begin to come in elsewhere, Maine is at its best.

The turnpike looks like an out-take from an old monster movie—a frantic stream of motorists converging on the state, as if to escape some unspeakable demon at home.

With summer come lakes and camps and beaches. Weekends take on an almost religious significance. Families unable to coordinate taking out the trash under normal circumstances, become combat ready with the warm weather. Picnics are packed, swim-stuff loaded, pooch in the minivan and they are off to the lake by 9:30 a.m. Saturday morning.

Summer is 26 days of good weather long. Everyone I know has a boat. I never used to appreciate summers much in Pennsylvania. (Okay, I promise I've learned my lesson!) I appreciate summer in Maine so much that I barely accomplish anything from July through August.

My weekends are spent with my favorite woman. We each get some "summer book" — actually, she reads about four of them in the time it takes me to read one. This year I am reading the Hunt for Red October. Last year it was a Stephen King book.

We gather our lawn chairs, coolers, floatation devices, snorkels, flippers, books, sunglasses, and anything else we need and head off toward Lesbian Lake, the mythical gathering spot for lesbians in Maine. Some women we only see during those 26 days of good weather each year. It's great for an update on the latest Women's (Womyns', wymmyn's, wymins's etc.) Music Festival. You know, did the showers work? Did you get another tattoo? Did it rain? That stuff. You get to find out who is living with whom, working at what job, moving to where.

New England is famous for being somewhat curmudgeonous. We tend to live our lives quietly and move in smaller groups. Bars and political rallies get boring after a while. It's nice to be able to see other lesbians in an arena where the biggest political question may concern the degree of sunblock to use.

But now I see by the calendar on my watch that we are approaching the second half of August. Soon September will arrive. Then October. I feel a bubble of panic rise from my solar plexus as I fight back images of alternately crying over and kicking the snow blower, woolly coats, and my broken defroster switch in my truck. I wonder if I will fix it this year or just turn the heat up full blast and alternately crack and close the window like I have the last year or so.

For this weekend, at least, it is summer at our house. We are having a deck built that may consume half of the back yard by the time we are done. The National Geographic Society has asked me to either mow the yard or declare it a national wildlife refuge. I may even pull out the weed-whacker and go crazy with trimming. Last time, I went through a yard of nylon cord, suffered approximately 57 cuts and scratches to my shins, collected 15 or 20 mosquito bites, and reduced the lawn to the equivalent of a marine crew cut. At least it was fun. After all, you only do it in the summer, right?

Last time, I finished the yard around 9:00 p.m. and sat down on the sidewalk to remove the many shaggy green lawn-bits from my legs before entering the house. I watched a pile of sidewalk ants.

They are the ones that make those tiny little sand mounds all over brick sidewalks. Their homes get scuffled over by pedestrians, squashed by bicycles, flooded by rains, fried in the heat, and yet they stand their ground. I wondered why they didn't just move a few feet over into the lawn. The grass there was green and cool, the food plentiful, and the livin' easy. The work had to be twice as hard, the food more-scarce, and security nonexistent where they were. Even more puzzling was the fact that since ants travel a great distance, they had to be able to see the yard.

Challenge. What is life without challenge? Maybe these ants, the ones working like slaves among the bricks, wanted something more. Maybe they thirst for the adventure and satisfaction that cannot come from the easy life.

Why do I live in Maine? Why do I not accept the mores of the *majority view*? Why have I chosen to not only take the path less travelled, but to shovel it myself?

I watched a dozen or so ants try to remove a little piece of mud obstructing the top of their hill. As a Good Samaritan, I removed it. They went crazy for a few seconds and went to another hill to perform the same function. I smiled and left them to their work...or play. After all, it was the weekend. And it was one of the 26 good days this summer.

A BOY NAMED SUE

1990 IS a year that I will never forget. I'll try really hard, but I'm afraid that this year – 1990 – with all of its "life-enriching experiences" (Oh, God! I'll never get through this!) And "personal growth challenges" (Why does this always have to happen to me?) will be one that sticks in my memory.

1990 was the year I sold out. Most people around me did not notice. Why? Selling out is a highly individualized and structured event.

I grew up in Northeastern Pennsylvania on a farm of around 100 acres. Our school bus driver was a local dairy farmer named Phil. Despite the snowy winters, he always got the bus through, often with a cheerful cry of, "we'll make 'er!" as the rest of us sat and prayed over the back axle to improve traction as we slithered along. We didn't have a radio on the bus back then so a couple of girls used to sing on the way to school and back every day.

Somewhere in the 70's, however, we got an eight-track player for the bus and Phil, who was crazy about Johnny Cash, played Johnny's two-volume, greatest hits tape over and over again for the next four years. There was one song in particular that stood out: A Boy Named Sue.

That's the tune about the young kid who is named Sue by his probably drunken father. Naturally, his life is one long series of fistfights and brawls as he tries to overcome his name. Somewhere in the fighting he finally understands that his father named him "Sue" in order to make a man out of him. His love for his father is restored. In closing, however, he mentions that if he ever has a son, he's gonna' name him Bill or Mark or anything but Sue.

As a lesbian, I can relate to that...sort of.

It is difficult for lesbians to both maintain a sense of identity and enjoy that identity in this society. Like making waves in a pool of water, we work constantly just to see the waves. We can't take a break and enjoy what we have accomplished. As soon as we stop making waves, the water's surface closes in and quietly erases all that effort. When you're fighting against society, momentum comes slowly. But if I let heterosexual society "make a woman out of me?" I will slip beneath the surface of those few waves left and disappear altogether.

I've spent 27 years bucking the system and it has made no noticeable dent in anything but my head. I've fought for 27 years against stereotyping only to find myself at 28 with a business suit and a skirt in my closet.

A skirt. If ever there was a lesbian white flag.

I might as well subscribe to Cosmo instead of surreptitiously snagging a copy at the check-out counter and attempting to hide it under a box of Cat Chow in case a lesbian comes by.

I am 28 and tired and just looking for a place to sit down. So, this is the year I officially sold out. I made a business suit. I planned it, went fabric and pattern hunting, put together something business-like but not too butch. Bought the pumps (God, those hurt!) and went to work.

I tried to rationalize this a hundred different ways: a business suit is just a uniform. Yeah, that's it. A uniform for work. Like a scuba suit or coveralls. Maybe if I put together the stereotype myself, it's not selling out. It's just satire. Or performance art. But looking at myself in the mirror in a skirt all I could think was, "Face it kid. You sold out."

I went to work. First hurdle was just trying to get into a pick-up truck in a skirt. Fortunately, the rip was tiny. Half way through the day I had a meeting downtown. Trying to walk quickly along brick sidewalks I discovered that even low heels do not mix with street grates. My feet were beginning to hurt.

Aside from that? I was treated like sheer royalty. No one called me "sir" for an entire day. I was afforded respect, courtesy, and friendliness everywhere I went. Seriously. I was amazed.

Oh, sure, I got a few complement-insults from women I knew, "See, you can be pretty when you just try!" Another woman, a total stranger, came up to me and engaged me in what I assume was "girl talk," commenting on my lapel pin. I didn't think she was cruising me...

Was this some kind of joke? The guy I saw every day in the parking garage. The one who never spoke to me, suddenly smiled and wished me a "good afternoon, young lady" He didn't recognize me in a skirt. Despite having dozens of encounters with him. Weird.

After work I stopped at the local grocery store. I moved slowly through the aisles like the Q.E. II, smiling as I quietly whimpered to myself in pain. Ten hours of wearing pumps. My toes felt strangely warm and numb...the way limbs feel right before an emergency amputation. I wasn't sure that I would ever walk again.

A child was yanked out of my path by his mother who hissed, "Get out of the pretty woman's way!" I couldn't stop myself from looking behind me, until I realized she was referring to me.

I was not allowed to carry my groceries to my pick-up truck by myself until I argued successfully that I only had two or three tiny items that would fit in a freezer bag.

Was this what it was like to be a heterosexual woman? Was this normal? It seemed like pure heaven. UNTIL.

Two lesbians were coming into Shop-N-Save as I was leaving. They both looked at me. I looked at them. I tried to smile innocently, sending a mental message of "it's not what it seems, really!" They rolled their eyes, gave a huff, and walked off. I felt horrible. Sell out.

I loved the attention I got from planet Heterosexual.

I went home, hung up the suit, and hunted for my flannel shirt. Kicked off the pumps and went deliciously barefoot. I was me again.

It was a pretty small thing when you think of it. Just a lousy business suit and a skirt. But somewhere in my soul I heard a cash register ring.

A VISIT FROM MS. NICHOLAS

'Twas the late eve of Christmas, when I unplugged the tree
And gave a smile to our goldfish in their two-gallon sea.
A crinkling of paper and a tiny pat, pat, pat
Alerted me to the threat of an incoming cat.
Gently I urged him, a pounce treat for lure,
But the tree gave a shudder, a streak of white fur.
Tossing the treat, I re-braced the tree,
And gathered the ornaments—at least those I could see.
Racing me up to the top of the stairs
I tripped on the damn cat, but couldn't have cared.
Into the dark bedroom, I tippy-toed in fright,
Hoping my eyes would adjust to the light
before I hit the bedside, the dresser or wall
I walked slow, like a zombie, my arms out and all.
Ah-ha! The bed I finally spied,
A beautiful woman asnooze at my side.
Her newspapers and paperbacks tossed onto the floor,
In a casual landslide that near reached the door.
Grabbing my bear, Steve, I made a cocoon
Of the down quilt and afghan–and planned to sleep until noon.
When out on the deck came a clatterous clank,
I figured in Portland, it must be a prank!

I stumbled out of bed to see if things were okay,
The window all frosty from heat leeched away.
Running half-blind I made it downstairs,
Searching for clues of the whos, whats, and wheres.
Outside a full moon cast a blue eerie glow
On the deck and the grill now covered with snow.
When what to my lesbian heart brought a pang But a woman in
red; my gosh, K.D. Lang!
A tiny black sleigh and guitar by her side,
I wondered if maybe she'd give me a ride...
Eight tiny reindeer, but, hell, who was counting
She commanded quite sternly as the sleigh she was mounting.
Her voice sweet and husky as she called them by name,
These big furry critters seemed reasonably tame.
"Now, Dasher! Now, Dancer!" a flash of a hoof,
"Holy Night," I thought, "she's goin' for the roof!"
To the top of the porch!"
"But, wait!" I then cried. "Take care near the gutters,
They're loose on one side!"
To the top of the porch, skipping the gutters,
They landed around the chimney and started to putter.
I dashed to the living room for no other reason,
Than it's stupid to stay outside when your fanny is freezing.
"What's going on down there?" My love was awake.
"Nothing, sweetheart!" I tried to placate.
A bit of coal dust and embers started to jiggle,
I couldn't stand the suspense and started to giggle.
With a puff of smoke K.D. Lang did appear
And I couldn't believe I was standing so near.
This was better than Star Search or A Current Affair.
No one would believe me, but what would I care!
The sack she carried was stuffed full of toys

For lesbian girls and gay little boys.
Records and gifts from the best of gay disco
Unavailable in stores, save for Boston or Frisco.
Magazines and hardcovers, and goodies you name it!
From the S&M shops where you buy it and tame it!
Gay guides that span your city or state
For those long business trips when you simply can't wait.
She sang not a tune but went straight to her work.
I stood dumbly staring. I felt like a jerk.
She filled all the stockings and patted the cat,
After giving a groan, on the couch she then sat.
As my eyes became more accustomed to the dark,
I started to think that this may be a lark.
It was then that I noticed the red high heeled pumps,
For a moment, I confess, she had me quite stumped.
Ever so slowly I was starting to see,
When she kicked off her pumps and said, "these are killing me!"
"This red and white outfit is really a drag!"
It was this remark that sent up the final flag.
"Why not add sequins, some color, say green?"
A lesbian? No.
This was Santa drag queen!
I stood looking stupid.
He said, "Dear, didn't you know?"
It was then that he gave a real "Ho, Ho, Ho!"
Getting to his feet and heading out of the house,
He said, "Best wishes to you, and of course to your spouse!"
"You're not using the chimney?"
"Oh no, that's a mess!
The first time I came down I ruined my dress.

LESBIAN PHONE SEX

"Mean Mommy Dearest looking for 'Bad Seed' to discipline. Will teach you how to be a little lady, whether you like it or not. No grano-las, bran-jockeys, or warm-fuzzies need apply to this Mama Superior. Send chalk outline and your worst nightmare to P.O. Box 6969, c/o Bitch Weekly."

No doubt about it. You don't see many lesbian ads in the personals section. Those few you do see fall into a few basic categories:

a. Totally well-adjusted, sincere, nurturing woman looking to open up and share inner-most thoughts and feelings with another serenely peaceful womyn, wymyn, woomun, what-have-you, while walking on the beach, picnicking, etc.

b. Prisoners looking for penitentiary-pals.

c. Heterosexual couples looking to fulfill a fantasy or two with the addition of another woman.

I have nothing against well-adjusted women, mind you. I've never met one, but I'd like to. Beach-walking and picnicking? Why do we always exalt these two testimonials to our serenity when most of us may actually do these one or two times a year—if we are lucky. Besides, I've never met any woman who nixed my beach plans in favor of organizing her spice rack, stacking wood, or cleaning the garage.

Once you get past the two or three lesbian personals, however, you enter a virtual Yellow Pages of gay personals. Words, abbreviations, measurements, and rules spell out graphically the ideal mate down to the very fantasy. Images like: Dungeon- master, greaser, panties-freak, two-somes, three-somes, two-tops-and-one- bottomsomes, leather, chains, Bondage, Tops, Bottoms, S & M. Only five-foot, blonde Asian men. Hairy. Hairless. Blue-eyed, double-jointed crossdressers. Masochistic transvestites into Epilady®.

Yeah, but does he like to walk on the beach?

Good grief! The Mary Tyler Moore in me rises slowly to the surface as I flip from page to page. Sometimes publications organize their fetishes you can just jump ahead to "*scatology*" to find your guy.

I've never made it more than half-way through any gay personals section. I put the magazine down. The next thing I know, I hear myself saying, "how about a picnic?"

I've never seen a photo of a *female* construction worker accompanied by a 900 number such as 1-900-PMS-DYKE. Or the classic "slightly damp *woman* without a shirt," sensually coiling the phone cord about *her* body. Call now—hot women are waiting to talk to you! [$2.00 for the first minute, $.75 for each minute thereafter.]

Surely the Lesbian community must have underground obscene videos. Where are all those nine-minute-long, grainy cinematic masterpieces with names like: "Bitch in Heat" or "Menstrual Hell"? Most attempts at *"lesbian porn"* that I've encountered read like a cross between *"The Well of Loneliness"* and transcripts from the Dinah Shore show.

I'm not helping things, either. I'll admit that right off the top. I'm a wimp.

Take a fantasy where some (adjective) woman slips me a note asking me to meet her at (location) for a night of pure (situation, in detail.) Okay. Now we're all set. My fantasy takes off okay, but before I know it, I find that I'm worried about being able to find that *location*, and—once there—a place to *park*. What if I show up on the wrong night. Or lose the note? Maybe I should make a photocopy of the note. Yeah, that's good. I'll stop at Kinkos. Uh-oh. Now there are two copies of the note.

What if this woman is married and her lover is insanely jealous? What if I have school that night? Is dinner included in *"situation, in detail?"* Should I bring something, like a bag of Cheese Doodles? How do they make those things anyway? What if she's into bondage? Or something really kinky.

What if she gave me the wrong note? Maybe she also gave her boyfriend a note that reads: I dented your truck. Call me at 555-9097.

Well, I got the Cheese Doodles, maybe I'll just rent a video and go home. The next time she sees me, I'll smile and speak Spanish. Or maybe I could move. Oregon is nice. I end up exhausted, stressed out, and grateful that it's over–before it ever started. Something tells me that this is not the manufacturers-suggested ending for an erotic fantasy.

Men and women are obviously different, but I can't figure out either of them. My version of Fantasy Island is neither a serene stroll, nor an X-rated scandal. My thoughts are less erotic and more neurotic. But my ultimate hot sex phone call?

Me: *dialing 900-HOT-LADY*

She: [ring] "Oh, baby...I can't wait till you get home. The bills are paid, the cat is fed, and I vacuumed the house."

Now that's a fantasy.

SEXUAL PREFERENCE VS CONDUCT

I WONDER if Governor McKernan got my letter. It was probably read by some Republican party flunky who drew the short straw. Or the new guy. I can just picture it...

A small, filthy office, a 60-watt bulb and pull-chain dangling from the center of a broken light fixture in the ceiling, bags overflowing with letters from Maine's gay and lesbian population, a water cooler filled with Pepto-Bismol. An exhausted figure hunched over a card table grumbles into a Dictaphone, *"Mrs. Myer...you got the address on this one? Okay. Take a letter. Dear so-and-so, thank you for your concern about LD 430 etc., but standard ending number 6. Sincerely yours, the honorable etc. etc. Dress it up a bit if you like."*

It was just an ordinary day. Got to work, made my morning cup of mint tea, checked my mail, and had all my political and personal freedoms denied.

In Augusta, politicians were declaring that a gay rights bill wasn't *necessary*. After all, there was no discrimination against gays/lesbians!

And we sure as Hellfire were not going to vote for a bill that would grant special privileges to "THEM."

Governor McKernan faced me at home via the six o'clock news and told me that in his *heart* he just couldn't justify that *"type of conduct."* His only option would be to send the bill to a referendum.

I think a similar theory was applied earlier in this country's history.

It had something to do with a scuffle between the North and the South.

Those around me kept coming out with comments like, "well, I don't care so much about that—I just don't want any homosexuals teaching my children."

I am tired of breast feeding a country that turns rabid at the first signs of change. I am fed up with nursing along those around me who "just can't—or won't—understand." I have tried to meet you more than halfway. I am exhausted.

And I want my money back.

Over the past few years I have paid $13,000+ in federal and state income taxes. This doesn't cover social security, health insurance, property, occupational taxes, sales taxes, vehicle registration, or any other taxes. Just federal income tax and state income tax.

I live in a state that does not represent me politically or personally and has stated quite clearly that it won't. The same goes for the federal government. Taxation without representation is one of the cornerstones of this country's foundation. In short, I am being charged for a service not provided. Twenty-something percent of my income goes right off the top to the federal and state governments.

If the United States does not wish to grant me the same basic human freedoms that the heterosexual population receives then we can simply add a refund box to the 1040's that will return all money collected from the gay and lesbian population.

I'm serious. And I could really use the $13,000.

Sexual conduct is not sexual preference. Conduct has no gender preference. So, what's the difference? (Heterosexuals are advised to clip this out and anchor it to the fridge with a magnet.)

Preference: Mark loves Bill.

Conduct: Mark and Bill purchase a mechanical bull, 6 gallons of whipped cream, and a metal detector for a fun weekend.

Preference: Susan loves Jim.

Conduct: Susan and Jim purchase a mechanical bull, 6 gallons of whipped cream, and a metal detector for a fun weekend.

Preference: Sandra loves Kathy.

Conduct: Sandra and Kathy purchase a mechanical bull, 6 gallons of whipped cream, and a metal detector for a fun weekend.

Any questions?

LESBIAN LEADING LADIES

GONE WITH *The Wind* came out in 1939. So did Scarlett O'Hara. And despite warring actors, the war between the states, discrimination, poverty, and those damn Yankees, *Gone with The Wind* remains one of the greatest lesbian love stories of all time.

What?

You heard me. Just look at the relationship between Scarlett and Melanie! Two Southern women who did not let some little old thing like the Civil War distract them from their true purpose – to stay together till death did they part. I'm not saying it was a perfect relationship, however.

The occasionally-ruthless Scarlett could not get enough of Melanie, a woman whose overwhelming goodness and purity would gag Mother Theresa. Melanie, a passive manipulator, loved the fire and spunk of Miss Scarlett – or should I say *Ms. Scarlett*. Scarlett was raw passion and daring. A woman who wouldn't let the death of her token husband, old *What's His Name*, keep her from hitting the dance floor once he was out of the picture.

Scarlett purged her inner demons through Melanie's sanctuarial and ever-forgiving nature. Melanie grew closer to Scarlett through these encounters, dipping into the dark side of her desires, and playing Ms. Scarlett like a finely-tuned instrument.

Intelligent and hungry for adventure, Melanie became weak and helpless when Scarlett showed signs of straying from Tara. While Scarlett kept cashing in her very soul to the devil whenever it seemed to Melanie that her work redeeming Scarlett was through. They could not leave each other alone. It was sadistic. It was masochistic. In other words, it was a successful marriage!

Any married person knows exactly what I mean. Just switch around a few words; "lawnmower" for "hoop skirt," or "grocery shopping" for "cotillion" and you'll find you've probably had similar, if not identical, conversations with your mate.

For those who swear their relationships are nothing but a walk in the park on a sunny day: think back to the last time the two of you tried to install a bathroom faucet, or check for radon in the basement.

Melanie and Scarlett had to play the game, of course, and those false-front, billboard marriages provided the perfect cover-up.

You could just see the personal ad in the **Atlanta Daily**!

Needed: one Southern gentleman, pref. charming, backbone of silly putty, indecisive and seldom home a plus. No Yankees. Respond to Ms. Melanie, temporarily staying at Tara.

Needed: one gambling rogue, morals of a viper, Yankees okay, workaholic and seldom home a plus. No sex. Respond to Ms. Scarlett, Tara.

Both came up with a close approximation, weeded out a few rejects, and then basically ignored both save for the occasional interaction necessary to keep the wondering public happy.

When it came to the really juicy issues, those women came together like thumbtacks and a magnet.

Scarlett did lapse into a straight period, during which time she gave birth to the required child only to find that she had now had Rhett Butler to look at every morning for the rest of her life, plus the responsibilities of motherhood.

She spent money like a drunken sailor, argued with Rhett, and became a public scandal.

Denial. Pure and simple.

We all know where Scarlett was when Melanie had *her* child. Verbal thrashings aside, Scarlett was the one true and dependable support in Melanie's life. Right to the end.

So, what about Ashley and Rhett? Frankly my dear, I don't give a damn.

Some people may argue my viewpoint, but when you're a lesbian, you take your victories where you find them. The pickins' can be pretty slim!

A little creative thinking can help to eliminate that creeping feeling that there really are less than 72 other lesbians on the planet.

How about that scene in Ghost where Patrick Swayze "borrows" the body of Whoopi Goldberg to enjoy a final embrace with Demi Moore? Demi cannot see Patrick, yet the audience does. So how come when Whoopi embraces Demi, it's Patrick we see—from Demi's viewpoint?

Yeah, right.

Of course, there's the recent L.A. Law ratings-booster which featured a kiss between lawyers C.J, and Abbey. Through the lesbian grapevine that news spread to every lesbian in America.

Like the night before Christmas, I couldn't get to sleep for a good couple of hours after the show. I was thrilled. I had waded through heterosexual soap operas, movies, TV shows, stories, series, commercials, videos, talk shows, news programs, sporting events, infomercials, and MTV. And had finally seen a lesbian encounter.

I only had to wait twenty-eight years.

Oh, sure, there have been earlier movie-of-the-week hints of lesbianism. Usually done badly. However, this was not a movie about lesbians and the fate that befalls the "lifestyle". This was simply an encounter between two women. An actual kiss!

I began counting backwards from ten, waiting for the flood of hate mail to show up in the TV Guide from angry religious extremists. I counted backwards slowly, waiting for the network to kill off one or both characters. But it didn't happen. And L.A. Law snagged me hook, line, and sinker.

The relationship began to bud between the two female attorneys.

Thursdays took on an almost religious significance. Then, just when I was thanking the cosmos for such a gift, the relationship was cut off in a way both clumsy and embarrassing.

In the words of L.A. Law, I object!

The next century will bring greater awareness, tolerance, and dignity. Those who took the risk in this century will be respected as visionaries before their time. Those who didn't will be remembered with all the other hate groups and collective injustices that burn shamefully within us.

I will keep watching L.A. Law. Maybe the lawyers—and writers, and directors, and producers will find it in their hearts to rekindle the flame.

After all, tomorrow is another day.

NOT IN MY FAMILY!

I'M JUST going to come right out and say it. I would swear that one of my parents is a heterosexual. Maybe both of them. I know it's not unusual to find at least one in your family tree if you shake the branches, but two? I know what you're going to say: "Don't jump to conclusions, Holly, it's not your fault!" That's easy for you to say. It's not *your* parents!

I really had my first clue at the age of five, when I began to absorb the layout of the house, both parents were sharing a single bedroom with only one bed. Oh, they were clever enough...making sure that there was always an extra bedroom in case "visitors" dropped by...but privately, they always referred to it as *the guest room*. Even when we moved they did the same thing. Putting together an extra bedroom and then the two of them *sharing a room*.

You're probably thinking that this alone is pretty flimsy evidence. Certainly not enough to justify slapping label on someone you love, but how do you explain the times that I'd come dashing home from school, head for the kitchen to fix myself the traditional after-school snack, and run smack into my parents hugging—or even kissing. It was definitely more than a friendly gesture. As I got older I noticed that my mother didn't spend a lot of time with women her own age, instead preferring to spend time alone or maybe just hang around with my father.

My father did have a good job rebuilding kitchens and baths. And he did work with other men. But when he had free time? He'd be somewhere around my mother. You could count on it. I did not know what to do.

I couldn't bring myself to ask my parents about it. Maybe I just didn't want to hear *that word*. For a while I considered asking one of my favorite teachers. Miss Homeroom.* I felt I could trust her not to blurt out anything in front of the class and effectively ruin my life. One afternoon when I was staying after school to attend a girl scout meeting, I got up the courage to ask. As I quietly walked into the classroom, I was horrified to find *her* in the company of my math teacher, Mr. Bicep*, in something more than an *educational capacity*. So much for asking either of them.

Being a precocious child, I obtained a copy of Everything* You Ever Wanted to Know About Sex, But Were Afraid to Ask. The chapter on heterosexuals was short, but the outlook for their unhappy lives seemed bleak and unfulfilled. No wonder they called them the "opposite sex".

Just as Doctor David Rubin had predicted, my parents were no longer getting along. Worse yet, I began to question my own sexuality. I was nearing puberty at the time and my brother was well into it.

The turmoil in our family increased and I watched helplessly as my brother succumbed to the influences of my parents. First, I found blatantly heterosexual pornography (Where do they get that stuff?!) under his bed as I was making my semiannual sisterly invasion of his privacy. Next, he began talking to me about *girls*. I was a nervous wreck.

Thankfully I wasn't as impressionable as my brother. I breathed a sigh of sexual relief when I became quickly addicted to a new television show called *Charlie's Angels*, and developed a severe crush on Jaclyn Smith. Even when the line-up of angels changed I managed to keep my cool and re-attach myself to Kate Jackson. I naturally hung out with girls of my own age at school and even managed to gain the company of women in the higher grades. When puberty came, our gym teachers wisely separated the girls from the boys. I, too, felt that kind of co-ed environment on a continuous basis would lead to trouble. At least I could say that *someone* in the family was *normal*.

Eventually my parents divorced. (See, I told you so! Those relation-ships never work out.) I hoped that they had learned a valuable lesson and would get on the right track. I didn't nag them about it. I figured that they were getting enough "how-do-you-know-till-you-try-it" pressure from their peers.

The weird thing is that they both sooner or later latched onto mem-bers of the respective opposite sex *again*. This time, however, they both seemed to be genuinely happy. With the added bonus of having moved away from the old hometown where everyone knows your business, they are now living *openly heterosexual lives.*

I can't really say that I understand it fully, but I respect everyone's right to do what they think is best. I guess having heterosexuals in my own family brought it home, so to speak, that a person's sexuality is just one small part of a very complex individual. It made me more compassionate.

My parents don't have any problem with me telling people that they are heterosexual...or as they like to call it, "straight." (Heterosexual does sound kind of impersonal.) One parent feels that there's nothing wrong with it and therefore no reason to hide it. The other doesn't really discuss sexuality much, but if you ask her about it, and, as she says, "you aren't just trying to give me a hard time," she'll tell you outright.

Oh, sure, it probably still shocks a few people. But all I can say is, "Hey, man, this is the 90s. Get with the program!"

* Names changed in case either is still closeted

CHRISTMAS TIMING

SEVERAL WINTERS ago, I remember an afternoon spent examining the frost tracks that crawled snail-like across the bay windows of our old farmhouse. The pattern started at the glass edges closest to the heater, fanned up and across the pane, and ended between the woodwork, allowing what little warmth our senile furnace could produce to escape quietly into the November day.

A neurotic wind tormented small drifts of twice-raked maple leaves, whirling a few into a crazed square dance, then tossing them off to spin helplessly into the lilacs, or raspberry brambles. Our house, built before the word "insulation" was coined, wheezed like a bronchial ward in a sanatorium. Each gust produced a rushing intake of loose panes, shutters, boards, and shingles that would explode in a spastic gasp, shaking the windows against the casings. Slowly, everything rattled back into place.

The mention of the holidays came up as my mother and I chatted that day. She gazed out the window, heaved a sigh and made some comment like, "I guess it's time to drag all that stuff out again." Poor woman, I thought. What a tragedy to see the old (she must have been all of 42) become crusty, curmudgeonly, no-fun Scrooges! I suppose life has finally gotten the best of her.

That will never happen to me.

Last week I was flipping my Beautiful British Columbia calendar from its September position to November, enjoying along the way the lovely October photo that I never had a chance to get bored with. I took a peek at December, did some quick math, and thought, "I guess it's time to drag all that stuff out again."

Oh my God.

Remember when the word "holiday" didn't naturally conjure up the word "stress". If you mixed two parts Normal Rockwell, with one part Dostoevsky (the Crime and Punishment period), and added a pinch of Woody Allen's Interiors, you'd pretty much have my family's version of the holidays. The last time we gathered as a family for the holidays, the stock market hadn't peaked 2000, Mork and Mindy was the hottest thing on TV, and Ronald Reagan was measuring his office to see if it really was oval.

Don't get me wrong. I love Christmas.

I love watching the local towns put on their version of the Nativity scene. You know, two wise men drinking coffee to ward off the cold while the third sits in the car on the verge of hypothermia.

Sometimes towns go the distance and hire a couple of real sheep for the occasion. Usually such efforts result in an evening spent trying to coax the critters into view from their cozy manger spot—or trying to keep them from wandering off into traffic.

I love the zeal with which people decorate: the tiny-candles-in-paper-bags that tastefully line the streets of Alfred every year, the local neighbors who go crazy and deck their halls with everything from reindeer on the roof, to a Santa stuck halfway down the chimney.

My favorites are the multitude of houses that began with good intentions but ran out of electric lights. A string of blinkers will start at the lower left edge; climb up and around a window, only to end abruptly in mid-pattern.

Last year I joined a Volkksport group for a 10K (that's 6-point-some-thing miles) evening walk around Falmouth before Christmas. The decorated houses looked wonderfully warm and cozy, especially after the first few "K's" in the cold. The last 45 minutes (what on earth possessed me to take on such a challenge?) found me wandering around in the dark on the verge of frost bite, flashlight batteries dimming, praying to either see the golden arches of McDonalds along route 1 (our destination point) or to be hit by a car. The walk took two hours plus, and like my one-day-guaranteed learn-to-downhill-ski adventure last year, I may never do it again.

The best part of Christmas to me is the joy of spending loads–no, oodles–of money on everyone. Probably because I've never been able to financially swing it. Someday, before I die, I hope to be wealthy enough to send a Harry & David Fruit of the Month Club to somebody.

Somewhere, somehow during my formative years, the Harry & David F.O.T.M. club got stuck in my psyche as the sign of ultimate wealth on the planet earth. Just imagine! Grapefruits, apricots, polished apples, all tucked in that green frizzly stuff. And a new box every month! I mean, who would normally pay twenty bucks for a dozen apples? They must be the most perfect apples in the world.

It should be remembered, however, that I was also thoroughly impressed by the fact that my partner (going back five years to our early days) actually had a coffee table in her house. A coffee table. A table that served no other use but coffee. At the time, my worldly furniture possessions consisted of two lawn chairs, a drawing table, three crates, and a futon.

This year's Christmas gift buying in Maine will probably feature gifts of electricity, water, and property tax lottery tickets. Maybe I'll buy a couple of gallons of heating oil to tuck under the tree. Or a gift certificate for the local Shop-N-Save. Perhaps a coupon good for one resume to be typeset on my Macintosh. Maybe just cash.

Maine's depression is going through the terrible-twos. Banks are being swallowed up like milk-duds, lay-offs and unemployment keep rising. Twelve months of watching CNN has left me with the neurotic desire to bury my money in coffee cans, stock up on food in bulk at the new warehouse-department stores, and finally pay off my credit card.

The thought of Christmas spending left me as depressed as the economy. At first.

But then I decided to look upon this holiday season as a challenge. I sat down and took a look at my Christmas list of family, friends, acquaintances, etc. Many of these people I seldom see. Phone calls, letters, and brief encounters are often spent giving a USA Today rundown of the past month, year, or decade: Chris got married, bought a house, bought a better house, had two kids, and just bought another dog. OH. Did I tell you about the satellite dish?

Time is really our most precious resource, yet we would rather spend money than time.

This year I am spending time. The gifts I am making–which account for about 90% of my list–have been underway since early November. Most are inexpensive, but carefully thought out. The real gift is the time spent in the making, thinking of the person for whom the gift is tailored, having them in mind at every step of the way. It's an unusual perspective in a world filled with Game Boys, Nintendos, VCRs, clothing, answering machines. Isotoners, Soloflex machines and thousands of other doo-dads.

And what do I want for Christmas? Well, there are the usual necessary things: blank diskettes for my computer, and maybe an evening with Jodie Foster. Among the more frivolous items? Maybe a computer diskette storage case, some blank diskettes, and perhaps an evening with Jodie Foster. In lieu of that, a little time spent with my partner, my cats, and my goldfish would be great.

With few people anxious to spend, and fewer people able to, this holiday season promises to be the best ever. If we all just take a little time to give a little time.

MEN & WOMEN–THE
COMPLEMENTING SEX

I SEEM to recall a health class in grade school sometime in the early 70s. We were still too young then to be separated by gender. We sat desk-by-desk, little girls and boys together. *Practically* touching.

The time had come for us to see *the film.*

An industrial steel-grey cart carrying a battered piece of equipment was wheeled into the classroom. Troy Elementary School had three film projectors, I believe. Each one suffered from an abnormality that caused the take-up reel to function smoothly for upwards of thirty seconds and then suddenly stop. During the lull, roughly five yards of film would coil snake-like to the floor in a dusty tangle. The take-up reel would suddenly spin back into action, madly rewinding not only the five slack yards but yanking the film feeding through the projector in a manner that caused the image upon the screen to hiccup. Sort of the cinematic equivalent of a *wedgie.*

The heavy rosin-colored shades were drawn, the movie loaded, screen pulled, and the lights dimmed. Hectic tidbits of image popped about the screen followed by the ten-nine-eight symbols. The film was entitled *The Miracle of Life* or something to that effect.

More in-depth than the fourth-grade warm-up *Bobby Has a New Sister* this film explored topics too gross for words. Like, sperm. Eggs. And how the two met. And what happened next. It was awful. Like a scene from a science fiction movie we watched a young and attractive middle-class couple chat (and hiccup) across the screen. Words were exchanged while standing near a car. A disembodied male voice offered a running dialogue of unmemorable chatter similar to, "blah blah blah, blah blah." Suddenly the camera zoomed in and before you could ask, "would you care for a glass of wine?" you were getting a cellular view of the couple becoming a threesome. A zillion swimming things were heading like salmon, upstream against terrible odds. At their final destination sat a quiet egg, all but unaware of the legions crusading toward her. Hundreds and thousands never survived the trip.

But one did.

Whammo! We watched in horror as things began to split, mutate, grow, and develop. This pre-dated the popularity of natural childbirth, so our next shot of the couple was a happy departure as they left the hospital with a tiny baby. The film ended and the lights came up. We sat dazed, stupefied, and terrified. No one raised a hand when our teacher asked if we had any questions. I rode home on the school bus thinking, *"you did that to MOM?!"*

I could not get the thought out of my mind. It was so clinical, scientific, and void of feeling. As if humanity roamed the earth in little blue business suits and sensible shoes by day, only to degenerate into raging fits of cell duplication and science experiments when the lights went out. It made the sexes appear to be so, *opposite*. As if normally men and women shared nothing in common. As if this ritual reproduction was caused by some external force. A full moon. High tides. Static cling? I had to find out more.

It's tough for parents to discuss s-e-x with their children. Strangely enough, my parents were surprisingly candid. So candid that I was left mortified.

Lesson number 13: never ask your parents about sex. I'm sure that thousands of therapists are making a healthy living off the neurotic children of parents who swore that they would be *totally honest* with their kids. But like the Carly Simon song, *"We Have No Secrets,"* I get the willies just thinking about it even today.

Okay, step two: ask my friends. Lesson number 14: never ask your friends about sex. That didn't take long.

How about an impartial adult? Lesson number 15: never ask a farmer questions about sex unless you are prepared to spend the next seventeen years trying to blot from your memory banks a menagerie of images of Holsteins, farm cats, woodchucks, and other rural critters passionately locked together in the throes of *heat.*

True, the examples were accurate to the concept, but... no one spoke of tenderness. No one spoke of passion. No one even spoke of *consent.* In an effort to provide the next generation with an *unbiased* sexual education that did not attempt to implant any particular morality, the adults of the world left out the most essential element–the only element upon which everyone agreed. *Love.*

In retrospect I think it was the biggest mistake ever made by our country's educational system. By defining us as opposite. By fostering confusion, frustration, and anger between the sexes through isolation. The last time I had gym class with boys was before I hit junior high. We had classes that were gender-identified. No girl in my school took "shop." It was a boys-only class. No boy took "home-ec" back then either. Our gymnasium had a pull-out dividing wall that was used when girls and boys were taking gym at the same time. We could hear them, but we couldn't see them. Somehow, once we flipped our tassels and stepped off the platform, diploma clenched in fist, we would supposedly rejoin the other half of humanity without skipping a beat. You can almost hear the chit chat at the grad parties, "Hello. I am a female. You must be a male." Is it any wonder that America is the number one producer of imprisoned sexual offenders throughout the industrialized world?

In some countries, a woman with a smaller-than-average dowry may be burned alive by her husband in order to trade up to a wealthier wife. Our country, in comparison, is Liberalsville, U.S.A. However, few surveys regarding gender in this country leave any woman with the desire to pop the cork on a bottle of champagne.

Men are paid more than women for equal work. It is documented all around us. Men are groomed for Chairman of the Board status while women are left behind in mid-management wrestling with a heavy workload and cranky photocopier. Men are allowed to age with distinction while the business world views a female executive with grey hair as little more than a bag-lady. Men are men while women are girls.

Flipping through the corporate photos of the Fortune 400 gives a very distinct impression that the world is run by slightly overweight, somewhat bald, middle-aged men. Those *opposite* men. It's enough to make us women want to light up a few flaming torches and head for republican headquarters, a NAPA dealership, or the local hardware store. That's where all the men are hiding, right? Time for a little payback.

And if all those men were misogynist bastards everything would be great. But they aren't. Just when I get fired up to do battle I come across nothing but *nice* guys. *Sensitive* guys. *Guys who understand my anger.* Guys who walked away in disgust from high- paying corporate jobs because they felt their female co-workers were being treated unfairly. Guys who work for the National Organization for Women.

Someone famous once said, "a house divided against itself never gets dusted." The Battle of the Sexes, like flag burning, is just that. A ticking time-bomb that explodes in a flurry of frustration and media hype that accomplishes nothing. Homelessness, drug abuse, poverty, depression, runaway taxes, serial murders, discrimination, natural disasters, global warming, ozone depletion, starving refugees, gang violence, pollution, and bank failures are too damn depressing to think about.

What we need is a good old-fashioned People magazine exposé like, *"Men and Women: Happily Ever After?"* We can probably ride it for a couple of weeks if we can get Geraldo to expose himself.

Maybe a few *Good Morning America* comparisons of how women are catching up to men. Throw in a few religious right-wingers while you're at it. That 'woman's place' stuff always gets them riled.

What a tragic waste of energy. Imagine the results if we put all that energy into oil painting or learning to speak Chinese. We'd be a nation of bilingual artists by now.

I am declaring myself a conscientious objector in the Battle of the Sexes. The first of many New Year's Resolutions for 1992 is to erase the word "opposite" from my mind. The new word is *"complementing."* The *complementing* sex. You may wish to break it in, so to speak, by using it for male-female occasions. In time, you'll find yourself using it in same-gender situations as well. Try it. When someone comes toward you, think of that person as the *complementing* sex. The tension begins to fade almost immediately. That battle line etched between the two of you begins to disappear to the point where you discover that you are both on the same side. You may find yourself looking forward to interactions that are female-male and male-female as a rare opportunity to "tune in" to natural rhythms that may not mirror your own. My personal goal is to eliminate my brain's constant need to categorize a complex and wonderfully unique humankind into boxes like: male, female, straight, gay, lesbian, bisexual, transsexual, etc. Why bother?

I couldn't come up with a good reason, either. Happy 1992.

THE 90S HAVE BEEN GOOD FOR LESBIANS

THE OTHER day I was on the phone with a male friend of mine (name withheld to protect the innocent) and we were discussing the changing nature of the gay and lesbian community.

Back when I first examined my sexuality, being a lesbian seemed to come with a lot of red tape, role-playing, and rituals. There were the *butch* lesbians, the *femme* lesbians, the *repressed* lesbians, the *granola* lesbians, the *political* lesbians, and that group of lesbians seen only in black and white photos. You know, they came in bunches, young, long hair, and usually frolicking around a country setting with their shirts off. If you research any lesbian anthology you'll find them scattered throughout.

My problem was that I didn't belong to any group. Picture *Mary Poppins* at a Hell's Angels heroin-fueled weekend. Butch was just not in my jeans. For some reason, the more femme I attempted to look, the more I looked like a drag queen after an all-nighter. One glance at my stash of Little Debbies, Marlboro lights, and back issues of Food & Wine magazine, and the granola lesbians wouldn't even grant me an interview. I'm cynical enough to believe that all politicians will become rotten to the very core if they stick around long enough and that stuffing envelopes is a job that will be waiting for me in Hell, so why spoil the fun now? It didn't make me the most popular activist among the political crowd. And I almost never frolic without a shirt.

The only thing I did have going for me was my cat, *Madigan*. Even he is a male. So where, I asked, are all the other non-conformist lesbians? I couldn't find them. For ten years through the Reagan 80s I searched with little success.

Suddenly, with the 1990s only two years old gay and lesbian themes have exploded all over the television from *Northern Exposure* to *Seinfeld* to *L.A. Law*. Suddenly, all those people who used to tell me that they'd be surprised if there was even one gay or lesbian for every 500 in the general population, are now asking me how many there really are.

A variety of hate-crime bills, police task-force units, legislative measures, employee benefits, and church policy discussions are now focused upon the rights of gay and lesbian citizens. I love it.

I love it because the boogie-person (boogie-man, boogie-womyn) of secrecy has been exorcised from our lives. The result is that lesbians, especially, are beginning to discover that they can be true to themselves without destroying community identity or existence. Without the constant need to reaffirm that "we are *here*," we can begin to define *who* we are—woman by woman and man by man.

But all of this is coming with a price tag for lesbians.

Last fall my partner and I decided to spend a rainy day shopping the outlets of Kittery. I remember the weather was bone-chilling and raw so it may have been late spring, or, summer, given Maine. Anyway, we moved from mall to mall with seven or eight thousand other people, leaving our bags at the front desk, being clicked in by the person counting the customers, waiting in lines, trying things on.

While my partner was on the never-ending crusade for women—trying to find a comfortable pair of jeans—I found myself entering an altered state. I wandered out of the store into an adjoining shop, poked around, and then wandered out. My face felt flushed and there were beads of sweat on my upper lip. My partner caught up with me outside and asked what I had purchased at the *Maidenform* outlet store, assuming that it was socks. She took a peek into the crumpled and sweaty bag.

What lurked inside was black, a fabric that was–dare I say it–slinky, with touches of–oh my God–*lace*. She stepped back and looked me straight in the eye. Was I on drugs?

My words came out choppy and confused, "I liked... these... so, I... bought a... pair."

The worst part is that I still like them! Holy soul-searching. Batman! No lesbian I know wears that kind of stuff–do they?

I've also noticed another bizarre trend. Back in 1980 I knew *one* lesbian who was allergic to cats. *One*. Each state had one, and she was the one for Pennsylvania. It was considered something of an oddity. Being a lesbian meant having *at least one cat*, but usually, several.

Anytime you travelled to the home of a lesbian you assumed that the place would be cluttered with cats. You might even be asked to *bring a cat to pass*. You know, B.Y.O.P.

Today I know three, maybe four, lesbians who are allergic to cats. My cat's patience is being stretched to the limit with temporary re-assignment upstairs or quarantine to my office when friends come to call. I've even heard lesbians complaining about *cat fuzz on their clothes*. What? I never saw this coming.

I won't even start on the bar scene. Lesbians in *dresses*? Pretty soon our "dyke spotting" weekends at the mall are going to level up to the Super Mario degree of difficulty.

I'm not saying that I can't handle it, or anything. It's just going to take some getting used to. Like, which goes better with my red flannel hunting shirt, the black lace bra or the hot red?

TOKEN LESBIAN

SNOW. SLEET. Rain. A 40% chance of gray. My truck sounds like it's trying to pass a kidney stone. There is water in my basement. My partner and I have spent the past three weekends crawling around on our hands and knees in our drippy basement tearing up asbestos floor tile in preparation of having the place waterproofed.

The floor, installed sometime during the bronze age, is welded in spots (floating in other spots) to the foundation in a loathsome soup that is two parts sticky black tile glue, one part reconstituted red paint, and three parts water seepage. I'd like to meet the guy who thought it would be a super idea to paint our cellar red... floor, walls, pipes. He's probably in an asylum for the criminally insane. Depending upon how long it takes to finish this job, I may meet him anyway.

Putty knives and hammers in hand, we pry, chip, and whack away for hours. I look across the room through scratched safety goggles and respirator at the woman I love. She is attacking, gladiator-style, the east corner with an ice chipper. Sweat puddles in my mask and images fill my mind. Pictures of me walking around this house five years ago saying, "hey, a little work here and there and this place will be fabulous!" I heave a sigh. Tile shards fly about like Chinese throwing stars, ricocheting off the furnace, the washer, and the two of us. I find myself doing things I never dreamed I would. Like wedging myself underneath a filthy oil tank to scrape out the weird shaggy stuff from a darkened corner. Finding myself overjoyed when I come up with a handful of composted tiles, dust bunnies, and what could be rodent remains.

Apartments start looking good. Real good. I try to remind myself that in fifteen or twenty years I'll have a good laugh about this. Once the foundation is exposed, our clothes are dropped on the spot for later detoxification. I take three or four showers and manage to get the majority of tile chips out of my hair. Is it spring, yet?

Another day breaks to Good Morning America and breakfast in bed with my lover and our cats. A public service message pops up during a commercial break. The voice over discusses A.I.D.S., but there is a photo of a man and woman kissing. Suddenly the photo switches to one of two *men* kissing. My spoonful of oat-bran pauses in mid-air. Another cut switches to a photo of two *women* kissing. My cereal bowl goes into my lap, my left hand clutches at my heart. I make sounds like a clogged sink. "Uh! Uh! Uh-uh…," I gurgle, pointing wildly at the TV.

The recent heightened visibility of the lesbian and gay community has had a profound effect upon me. I feel positively resurrected from a purgatorial state of non-existence and thrust into living color.

L.A. Law has a bisexual lawyer and recurring lesbian theme. The film Fried Green Tomatoes was one of the first lesbian-based films for the general public that did not constantly analyze the fact that the leading women were lesbians. A recent newspaper article about a kid who dropped out of school because he was hassled for being gay actually ended with him returning to a cheering group of classmates.

I was stunned. I don't even want to picture how that story would have ended back when I was in high school.

However, despite the media, I still seem to be the only lesbian in the lives of many straight persons I know. The token lesbian. Responsible for raising the consciousness–single-handedly–of many heterosexuals in my life. Parents, relatives, casual acquaintances, co-workers, and friends often claim that they never knew a lesbian before I walked into their lives. Or check-out stands, offices, Christmas parties, or, more recently, hardware stores.

Or maybe they think they know a gay man, but they aren't sure. Or the lesbian that they did know died of old age and now they need a new one.

Being the token lesbian is a full-time job with no overtime for holidays. It's a job that requires a backbone of cast iron for those times when some guy angrily walks up to you and starts talking about God, or why his ex-wife left him. And whether I know that "damn woman named Barb." Or those times when some child comments during a holiday dinner upon the nature of your relationship with his aunt. It's a labor of love in the truest sense of the word.

Or at least it was until February 17,1992.

Stopping at Shop-N-Save Monday for cat treats, Kleenex, and light cream, I came across a Newsweek cover asking, IS THIS CHILD GAY?"The article concerns the findings of neuroscientist Simon LeVay of the Salk Institute in LaJolla, California. In examining the cadavers of 41 individuals, 19 of whom were homosexual men, he found that a small area of the brain—the hypothalamus (believed to control sexual activity) was less than half the typical size in the gay men as opposed to the straight men. Interesting, but open to a lot of more scientific scrutiny and debate.

The rest of the article, however, was a hodge-podge of Sigmund Freud's theories on the origins of homosexuality, success stories of therapists who have cured gay clients, the possibility of a gay gene and the threat of genetic tampering. There were also a few personal stories including one woman who claimed that *had she been able to determine in advance that her child was going to be gay, she might not have carried that child to term.*

I'm sure some editor at Newsweek believes that this is a well-rounded and meaty study of gay and lesbian culture. It's not. It's a token. Token commentary by a few lesbians and gays stirred into an overabundance of heterosexual prejudice masquerading as news.

I absentmindedly began searching for the Ibuprofen.

What next? Budweiser commercials featuring T-shirts emblazoned with the logo, "Ask me about my hypothalamus!" Born-again heterosexuals? Prenatal screening for queer babies? The religious right might suddenly find themselves pro-choice overnight.

I would also like to know why the commentary by lesbian editor Frances Stevens appeared with a photo of her in bed with a pet pig minus any caption that would have explained just what the Hell she was doing. It always warms my heart to see articles featuring gays and lesbians engaged in counter-culture, whacko, or new wave activity. Why? Because I, *token lesbian*, will spend the next few months trying to convince twenty or more straight people that pigs are not the national symbol of gay pride, lesbians do not collect pigs, there is no pig-lesbian connection of which I am aware, and that the woman just had, I guess, a pet pig. Why? I don't know.

The article spotlighting condescending therapists who plugged their heterosexual-retraining programs were especially touching. I get all Thelma and Louise just thinking about it. I'm glad they didn't dilute the message with the conflicting opinions of those who are sane.

This is going to go into overtime. I can already hear three or four people I know saying, "well, in Newsweek that guy was queer...and he's normal now."

In focusing on the psychiatric community as a whole, the article did mention the *new* trend in therapy to not "cure" homosexuals, but to help them feel better about their existence.

Despite the fact that the American Psychiatric Association and its members removed homosexuality from its list of emotional disorders in 1973, 37% of the A.P.A. voted against that move a year later. Of course, that was then and the percentages have no doubt changed, but this article certainly didn't bother to look into that. The cure-the-homo story got the bold type on page 52 of Newsweek, reflecting a media still more interested in selling the "I was a teenage faggot" story.

Did I mention that the whole Newsweek article barely mentioned anything about LESBIANS? Save for the mention that Freud was always foggy on female sexuality. So, what we are left with is–let me make sure I get this right–upwards of 30% of the psychiatric community labels us as emotionally disturbed, while around 70% of the psychiatric community tries to make us feel better about the first 30%.

Something like a Ku Klux Klan fund-raising picnic where most of the profits go toward helping Blacks cope with the persecution and oppression of living in America, while a few dollars are put into a slush fund for sheets and dry cleaning.

I don't know that my opinion of the psychiatric community is improving any, but my feelings toward them are certainly growing stronger every day!

I think I'll take all that money I was going to blow on therapy and invest it into evenings out, champagne, a world cruise, college education, and a tune-up for the truck.

WCSH television evening news the other evening headlined a story about gay bashing and hate crimes. Oprah Winfrey's show that same day featured angry wives who decide to have it out with their husband's gay lovers.

It's all tokens. Token political-correctness. Token coverage. Token news item. Token issue. Token concern. There are countries so anti-female that the birth of a female child may easily lead to that child's murder by drowning or suffocation moments after birth. China and India are two examples of that kind of thinking. Strangely, we find that unconscionable.

In the United States, however, a mother professes to love her child enough that, if she knew she was giving birth to a gay or lesbian child, she would end the pregnancy. No doubt out of token love.

OUT AND ABOUT

How IMPORTANT is it that I am a lesbian? It's important to me, of course. But how important is it that *you* know?

There are plenty of things that you don't know about me. I have a compulsive habit of checking my emergency brake every few minutes when I am driving to make sure it is not engaged. I hate short sleeves but always roll up my long sleeves.

I was raised on a farm in Pennsylvania where my father, mother, brother, and I took care of several neurotic sheep, a handful of deranged chickens and dozens of farm cats. I graduated first in my class from high school.

I was raped when I was around 21. I worked as a night-shift D.J. for seven years. I've been writing for *Our Paper* for around five years.

Somewhere in all that I am also a lesbian. A lesbian who has never been in the closet.

The protest surrounding the Oscars and the rumors that Jodie Foster may be outed on television during the show is obviously global in reach considering that it has actually trickled down to my ears. I've sort of made a hobby out of being perpetually uninformed about social trends, goings-on, and gossip in general. If it weren't for the fact that I live with someone who reads the paper every day, my only social infusion would be from National Geographic, Food & Wine, and the Funny Times.

The process of outing celebrities and politicians enrages me. The outing side claims it to be a necessary evil in the battle to overcome homo-invisibilis and homophobia, and that those persons outed are, basically, so famous and /or wealthy that their lives have become the equivalent of shareware upon which the public hardware may chew.

"Hey, did you hear about Senator Spendmore?

"Yeah, wasn't his picture on a placard that read 'QUEER TO THE BONE' at the Capitol?"

"Yeah, boy that really tossed aside many of inconsistencies regarding the nature of our gay and lesbian citizenry!"

"Me too! I never fully appreciated the legitimacy of the lesbian/gay human rights issue. I think I'll go jot down some ideas for a piece of legislation that will have global implications!"

"Hey! Get that baby on my desk pronto! I want to add my signature as soon as possible so that we may swiftly move this through the legislative process!"

Hmmm. Call me a *pessimist*, but I don't think the results are going to be as positive as the Outers may believe. They do believe that the process will result in a positive and happy ending, don't they? I mean, they wouldn't plant a land mine like that and just walk away from the chaos, would they? I'm assuming that they have some kind of safety net? Support groups, funding, security, and a tag-team of therapists to help deal with the results of their work? Results like loss of income, family strife, parental custody cases, threat of personal harm.

Not to mention the general paranoia that results when a group out of nowhere decides to focus all their energies upon you. Think about the last time a few Hari Krishnas made a beeline for you in an airport, or the time when a handful of Jehovah's Witnesses showed up on your porch.

"Wow! Did you see the Oscars last night? They outed Jennifer Hollywood."

"It's about time someone knocked some sense into the heterosexual population! I loved Jennifer Hollywood in all those After School Specials about the Campfire Girls!"

"At last! A positive lesbian role model for my daughter! She's only 12, but I think she may be a lesbian!"

"Just like her older sister! That's great! America sure is a melting pot of social and ethnic diversification!"

I'll say. And thank goodness! I think we'll all breathe easier when we convince those less secure that individuality is encouraged in the U.S.A."

"You can't imagine the sigh of relief I let out when I discovered that my son's gym teacher is gay. At least I know my son won't be bombarded by constant heterosexist propaganda!"

"Amen!"

I consider myself to be a relatively private person. I shy away from crowds, seldom attend parties, and tend to suffer anxiety attacks at the Maine Mall when some department store employee approaches me with an application for a credit card in one hand and a free gift in the other. I spend the majority of my time working alone, with an occasional cat companion. My nearest relative is 500 miles away and we haven't seen each other in around ten years. I don't like telephones. In fact, if there were a lesbian monastery that had a big screen TV and a satellite dish, I would be wearing a saffron robe by now.

"Did you hear about Peter's ex-wife Helen?"

"I heard on CNN that she's a lesbian!"

"Yeah! Who would have thought? It's a good thing that she's got the kids. This should really be enriching for them, especially in these formative years."

"How old are they anyway?"

"Jane is four and Marc is just turning two."

"Lucky kids. At least they won't be raised to discriminate on the basis of sexual orientation."

A sadomasochistic virus has infected this country. Almost any night on television you may tune into a real live killing, or near death, or violent encounter during prime time.

TV offers us everything from Rescue 911 to jaggedly-filmed cop shows featuring such intensities as actual vomiting to massacres. It's a nationwide case of roadkillitis that propels us to hit and run over anything minding its own business, and then back up to get a good look before speeding off for more excitement, more confrontation, more blood.

I believe that my sexual orientation is nobody else's business. Hell, between working 50-plus hours per week and restoring our house, half the time it's not even my business.

Intimacy becomes exploitation when exposed to the public, like film exposed to sunlight. Accountability and responsibility distinguish the House of Lords from the Lord of the Flies.

"Frank! I just heard that Bill Clinton puffed on a joint (but did not inhale) while on a trip to England several years ago."

"My God, Susan, you are incredible. We've got to lead with this one! Can we get a graphic from production of a joint to super-impose on the photo?"

"No sweat, we can use the one from the Dan Quayle piece."

"Fabulous! What's the current lead?"

'Some group just outed Hillary Clinton." 'Hmmm. Let me think. Maybe we can tie these together..."

Note: *I voted for you, Hillary.*

NO SPECIAL PRIVILEGES REQUIRED

EVERY TIME I drive past the YMCA, I find my stomach muscles tightening up a bit. Strange that they should do that now. It wasn't all that long ago that I used to swim regularly in the upstairs pool three days a week.

I'd race over after work praying that I would be able to find a parking place amidst the chaos of parents dropping off and picking up kids.

The instructional pool was all but vacant at that hour. My only regular companions were a couple of older men who would do a few ceremonial laps, log rolls, belly flops, what-have-you, before wishing me a good evening and wandering back into the locker room.

The lifeguard on duty would look up occasionally and smile as I swam back and forth. It was wonderful. All those lines on hold, people asking questions, where's-my-whatever would disappear beneath the rippling waves of blue and quiet. I loved it.

My partner and I visited the YMCA on a regular basis—or tried to. Nautilus, swimming, and racquetball were our favorites. We did the usual thing. Exercising like crazy for a while then slacking off for a while, but all the time Casco Northern Bank was deducting a monthly electronic payment that would show up on my account statement. One of my favorite things about the YMCA was the fact that, as anyone who frequents a Y knows, at least 30% of the customer base is either gay or lesbian. Half the time we were there, the gay/lesbian population outnumbered the straight population.

But the day came when a friend mentioned that she was looking into a family membership at the YMCA for herself and her partner. The initial feedback she got left her feeling it would be okay. Since our single memberships together totaled more than a family membership, I figured it was worth a shot.

Working my way through the hierarchy of YMCA management I calmly stated that my partner and I would like to switch our single memberships to a single-family membership.

CONFUSION.

"What did you say your last name is?"

I told them.

"And what's the other name?"

"And you want what?"

I told them.

More confusion.

"A family membership is for families."

"We are a family."

"No, I mean married couples."

"We are married."

"And what did you say the first name is again?"

I told them.

"And the other person's name?"

I told them.

"Can I put you on hold?"

Like a Super Mario game, I worked my way up through the degrees of difficulty from secretary to assistant to assistant manager to manager. Each time the conversation was the same. Until I reached the top.

"You have to have a valid wedding license to get a family membership. You'd have to bring it in with you. A valid Maine wedding license."

"Do you require that all couples applying for family memberships present their valid wedding licenses?"

ASTONISHMENT

"No. Of course not."

"Then why do I have to bring in mine? I've told you that we are married. We share the same address. We have been supporting members for years and would like, under your new pricing system, to apply for a family membership."

This is when the facade began to crumble. "Look, we're a family organization. We are looking to attract certain types–families."

"I understand. We are a family. We have a house, two cars, two cats, and goldfish."

There was some sputter as the voice on the other end of the phone fought for control. I could hear the Bigot churning underneath the surface, flustered, trying to spit out words like "queers," while the Executive was trying to not create an incident by repeating over and over that I would have to present *a valid Maine wedding license.* And although we didn't hang up on each other, we might as well have.

I sat there with my hand welded in anger to the receiver. I could just picture this guy in his office with his hand on his receiver, thinking, "why do you people keep ruining my heterosexual day with your flagrant, immoral demands. You know we don't want your kind!"

"Doesn't this guy realize that the YMCA is a regular jungle gym for lesbians and gays?" I thought. It's like a counterculture ant farm with free weights. Look in any room and there are queers on the Nautilus, on that downhill skiing machine, in the swimming pools, working out on the stair-steppers. They are everywhere. The place is crawling with them. If the gay and lesbian population of America stopped going to the YMCAs and YWCAs the revenue loss would go down in Y history books as year they had to downsize to lower case letters.

At first, I figured, "Just try and keep me out!" Maybe if I refused to go away they would have to accept me sooner or later. Or, maybe I would just end up giving $400 yearly to a man who had insulted my partner and me. Year after year I would be supporting an organization that gave me the official, *"we don't want any trouble,"* the statement that always seems to come across more as a veiled threat than a diplomatic gesture.

Going to the YMCA didn't seem as much fun after that. I stopped swimming altogether. Exercise wasn't even necessary as I found that my blood pressure and my heart rate increased just by entering the building. It wasn't long after that I found myself depressed, and called the YMCA, canceling my membership.

I was left wondering, "why do you people keep ruining my lesbian day with your flagrant immoral demands?"

I'M A FRIEND OF RONALD R.

MY NAME is Holly...and I'm a Republican. I haven't voted Republican in at least the last two major presidential elections. My memory isn't so good before that time... You know, blackouts. Or, as we call them in Republicans Anonymous, *recounts*.

As you can guess, election years are really Hell for me.

My story is not unique. I came from your typical middle-class Republican background. My father worked a variety of jobs from sign painting to carpentry work. My mother worked at home as a writer. We looked like Democrats. We lived like Democrats. As far as the outside world was concerned, we were Democrats. Nobody had a clue that behind the curtains of voting booths all over Towanda, Pennsylvania, we were voting Republicans.

How did it all happen? Well, like many A.C.O.R.s (Adult Children of Republicans), I was raised in a Republican household. It simply was my political experience from day one. I didn't know any better. Besides, there didn't seem to be anything wrong with being Republican. It's not like my dad came home roaring in debate from an all-night rally in town, leaving a trail of Nixon stickers and buttons in his wake. My mother did not stumble out in front of my neighborhood friends with a handful of pamphlets—or show up at Croman Elementary School with a G.O.P. banner. They didn't stage violent political arguments at home. They were closet voters. Sometimes I wonder if, in some ways, that was actually worse.

Because the behavior was not extreme the problem was ignored much longer.

As I got a little older, I found myself hanging out with an unusual mix   of

teenagers. We debated together, played our own merciless version of Monopoly, and followed the stock market. During political seasons we staged our own "mock" elections. At the time we didn't know just what it was that drew us all together. I have since found that many of those high school friends became full-fledged Republicans.

I got my own crummy apartment and lousy job after high school and moved into town. At last! I was old enough to vote. And did I! Every primary, every election, from dogcatcher to President of the United States. I was the first one at the polls, magic marker in hand. I'd grab a crisp clean ballot...sometimes they were so new that they smelled like the dittos run off the ditto-master at Troy Senior High School. I would drink in the fragrance as I entered the booth and drew the curtain shut around me. What power! For a moment I could forget about my poverty-line existence and my meaningless life. I had a ballot in my hands and the rest of the week was going to be magic.

For years it went on this way. Withdrawal between Presidential elections, followed by a type of political binging that not only destroyed my life but also embarrassed and caused pain to many people who knew and loved me. Oh, it's not like they didn't try. Attempts were made to get me into volunteering for Jimmy Carter.... There was no stopping me. I was not in control of myself.

I am now strong enough to face my previous behavior and, having made a merciless inventory of myself, I have begun the process of apologizing to all those Democrats against whom I voted. I'd like to start with Mr. Carter. I'm sorry, Jimmy. And I'm sorry for the joke I made about the solar panels on the top of the White House. And the stuff about your brother.

It was during the Ronald Reagan years that it all came to an ugly head. A $100 per-person rally was wrapping up at a local country club. On my salary that was over half a week's pay. I couldn't get in. I hung around outside, picking crinkled red white and blue paraphernalia out of the dumpster; torn bumper stickers, dented buttons. Thinking maybe I would find a T- shirt or a baseball hat.

Somewhere in all that propaganda I blacked out.

The next face I saw' was an older man, trying to get me to move along. "What are you doing in the trash?" he asked, "Does being a Republican mean that much to you?"

I looked up. Dizzy and confused. I fumbled for words, "you don't understand. There's no high like it. Being on the side that *wins*. And... the parties after the vote is counted—the Republicans have *open bar*. The Democrats have B.Y.O.B.

He looked thoughtful for a moment and then fumbled around in his pocket for something...a card. He handed it to me. It looked like this:

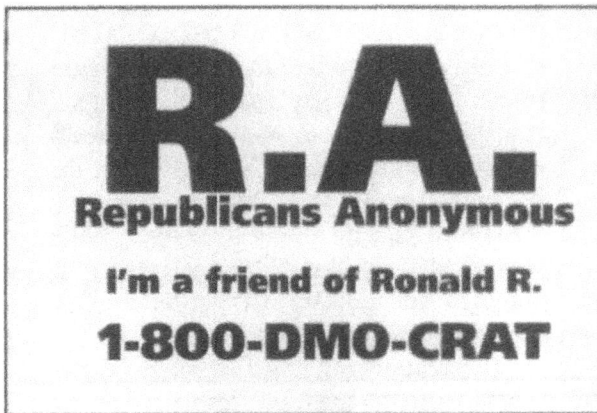

R.A.
Republicans Anonymous
I'm a friend of Ronald R.
1-800-DMO-CRAT

I called the number and got the help I so desperately needed. I have been GOP-free now for several years, with the help of my sponsor, George Mitchell. Some of my old friends have even attended POLI-NON, in support of my struggle.

This year's election will bring out the same compulsive desires in me at the polls. I'm sure, but I think I'm strong enough to do the right thing. As we say in R.A., I just take things *one ballot at a time*.

BETTER NEW YEAR'S RESOLUTIONS

How DID New Year's resolutions get such a bad rap?

Whether it's a promise to stop compulsively surfing up and down the radio dial at the first hint of a commercial, or an honest effort to re-fit your Tupperware containers like those Russian dolls to save on cupboard space, people just don't take to resolutions much anymore. No matter how small the change.

In fact, whenever I ask anyone what resolutions they've made (those resolutions that are fit for polite conversation) they usually look at me as if I've just sent them a chain letter—or volunteered them for an IRS audit... Why?

The word "resolution" means: 1. The state or quality of being resolute; firm, determination. 2. A course of action determined or decided upon. 3. An explanation, as of a problem or puzzle; a solution. 4. The action or process of reducing something into its constituent parts: the prismatic resolution of sunlight into its spectral colors.

Sounds pretty good when you put it that way.

Yeah, but we all know that resolutions always mean giving up something we love—-like chocolate or cigarettes. In the glow of a champagne-steeped New Year's

Eve we publicly announce to friends and family that we are going to eat more leafy- green vegetables, give up the hard stuff, and get to bed by 10:00 p.m. every night— starting next year. The morning—and year—after brings guilt, embarrassment, and the joy of knowing that for the next couple of weeks those present at your public proclamation will call you on the carpet every time they see you leaving a bar at closing time or nibbling junk food.

Rule number one is realizing which resolutions warrant a public announcement and which should be kept private. For example:

    a. A promise to cut back on your heroin habit

    b. Learning how to ski

    c. Changing religions from mainstream to cult

    d. Telling friends that you are an extraterrestrial from a distant galaxy

    e. Learning how to cook seafood

    f. Giving up a life of crime

Answers "B" and "E" are public resolutions. Answers "A", "C", and "F" are private resolutions. The trick question is "D". If you find yourself at a Star Trek convention, have at it! At your therapist's office is a maybe... It's amazing how many people will keep a resolution to get out to the movies more often a guarded secret while telling everyone within earshot that they are seriously planning a sex change.

The success or failure of many resolutions begins and ends here.

Rule number two is to pick resolutions wisely. For example:

List 1

    a. Drink more heavily

    b. Smoke unfiltered cigarettes

    c. Pirate HBO Cable

List 2

    a. Lose 80 pounds

    b. Take up Olympic gymnastics

    c. Give up television

Neither list is acceptable. Extremism, illegality, and practicality must be taken into consideration along with quality of life. A better mix might include:

List 3
    a. Eat less junk food
    b. Visit friends more often
    c. Take a crack at physics
    d. Improve parallel parking skills

Rule number three is to under-promise and over-deliver. A resolution to cut back to one pack a day is probably more successful than repeated attempts to go cold turkey. Remember, too, that everyone experiences *malfunctionus resoluticus.*

One year I made a private resolution to learn how to ski. Despite the fact that I was over 25, out of shape, and had no natural inclination toward anything more athletic than backgammon, I decided that skiing certainly looked easy, and, therefore, must be something that I could learn. I really wanted to learn, too. I was up for it!

You know, a great winter sport in Maine! However, my one day guaranteed-learn-to-ski adventure at Sunday River quickly turned from being step one toward my dream of becoming the next Thrill of Victory to a masochistic ritualized form of humiliation and embarrassment that left me covered with dodge-ball sized bruises and curled up in the fetal position by 7:00 p.m. that evening under the covers.

I'm not sure, but I may have even resorted to thumb sucking. For weeks I would go ashen every time I saw that damnable skiing weatherman on TV.

Two years later I am not only over that incident, but I am prepared to ski again. Oh, not outside, mind you. As a matter of fact, if I ever make a move to take this body—now over 30—to the top of a snowy mountain, strap a couple of slippery boards onto my feet, and jump off I hope somebody on the chair lift puts a ski pole right through my heart.

I'm talking about our new NordicTrack Pro. Best damn exercise in the free world— according to their brochure. Now I can watch the Skiing Weatherman and ski along with him! Best of all, in just a month or so you can be in primo physical condition, assuming that you don't blow a heart valve with that full-body workout! So, this year, my public resolution is to figure out how to use the thing without breaking a bone and maybe even ski a couple of kilometers over the course of 1993.

Privately? Well, ABC has been running that Thrill of Victory/Agony of Defeat spot for an awfully long time. Maybe I should set up the camcorder...

30ISH YEARS LATER

CHANGE DOESN'T take time. Change happens in a *flash*. What takes time is the *geological grind* of status quo that precedes change. For older lesbians like myself, that grind was half a century. For Millennials it took *weeks*.

During that grind a few relationships emerged. Some fizzled. A few exploded. Then I met Janet. In 27 years of living in Maine, we've gone through two houses, a dog and two cats, ice storms and blizzards, and more trips to Home Depot for plumbing parts than I can count.

Somewhere in between furnace repairs and trips to the vet, change suddenly happened. Society caught up. We became **cool** – really cool – if much older.

Now I see lesbians on TV ads. I don't know how many times I've watched Black Mirror's San Junipero episode. I was stunned to see a recent episode of ABC's Stumptown feature investigator Dex Parios (Cobie Smulders) in a lesbian one-night-stand. I felt *exposed*. I viewed my life as purely political for so long that seeing cultural representations of everyday lesbians shocked me.

But I'm loving it. And it's a great time to be an older lesbian.

I distinctly remember passing my physical prime somewhere between knee replacements one and two. But I don't know that I've hit my intellectual prime or spiritual prime yet. Is there more than one prime?

57 is not a prime number, but it is a *semi-prime* number. So, even if I missed my one and only prime, it's got to be close by. Stay tuned.

ACKNOWLEDGMENTS

I would like to thank my long-suffering friend and editor Elizabeth Isele for finally drilling into me how to properly format an en dash. Or was it an em dash? *Damn.* Her expert guidance, proofreading chops and sincere enthusiasm are largely responsible for this 30-year project finally crossing the finish line.

I would also like the thank Susie R. Bock, Coordinator of Special Collections, and Director of the Jean Byers Sampson Center for Diversity in Maine at the University of Southern Maine for her support and assistance while I was trolling the digital collection of *Our Papers* at the Portland campus, comparing digital editions with my musty physical copies.